JOB AIDS
Basics

JOE WILLMORE

A Complete, How-to Guide to Help You:

✓ Understand Basic Principles and Techniques

✓ Create and Use Job Aids Effectively

✓ Enable Top Performance

ASTD Press

ASTD Press is an internationally renowned source of insightful and practical information on workplace learning and performance topics, including training basics, evaluation and return-on-investment (ROI), instructional systems development (ISD), e-learning, leadership, and career development.

Ordering information: Books published by ASTD Press can be purchased by visiting our Website at store.astd.org or by calling 800.628.2783 or 703.683.8100.

Library of Congress Control Number: 2005939036

ISBN-10: 1-56286-415-7
ISBN-13: 978-1-56286-415-6

Acquisitions and Development Editor: Mark Morrow
Copyeditor: Karen Eddleman
Interior Design and Production: Kathleen Schaner
Cover Design: Ana Ilieva
Cover Illustration: Lael Henderson

Printed by Victor Graphics, Inc., Baltimore, Maryland, www.victorgraphics.com.

Table of Contents

About the
Training Basics Series

■ ■

ASTD's *Training Basics* series recognizes and, in some ways, celebrates the fast-paced, ever-changing reality of organizations today. Jobs, roles, and expectations change quickly. One day you might be a network administrator or a process line manager, and the next day you might be asked to train 50 employees in basic computer skills or to instruct line workers in quality processes.

Where do you turn for help? The ASTD *Training Basics* series is designed to be your one-stop solution. The series takes a minimalist approach to your learning curve dilemma and presents only the information you need to be successful. Each book in the series guides you through key aspects of training: giving presentations, making the transition to the role of trainer, designing and delivering training, and evaluating training. The books in the series also include some advanced skills such as performance and basic business proficiencies.

The ASTD *Training Basics* series is the perfect tool for training and performance professionals looking for easy-to-understand materials that will prepare non-trainers to take on a training role. In addition, this series is the perfect reference tool for any trainer's bookshelf and a quick way to hone your existing skills. The titles currently planned for the series include:

- ▶ *Presentation Basics* (2003)
- ▶ *Trainer Basics* (2003)
- ▶ *Training Design Basics* (2003)
- ▶ *Facilitation Basics* (2004)
- ▶ *Communication Basics* (2004)
- ▶ *Performance Basics* (2004)
- ▶ *Evaluation Basics* (2005)

- *Needs Assessment Basics* (2005)
- *Return on Investment (ROI) Basics* (2005)
- *Organization Development Basics* (2005)
- *Coaching Basics* (2006)
- *Change Basics* (2006).

Preface

■ ■

When I first began work as a trainer, I was initially surprised at how useful and effective job aids always seemed to be. Starting out in training, perhaps I was guilty of assuming that if a solution didn't involve formal, structured training as a means of passing on knowledge, it couldn't be effective. Additionally, I really couldn't appreciate the value of something that can be as simple as a laminated piece of paper small enough to fit in a shirt pocket.

In any case, early in my career I tended to view job aids as primarily adjunct or support items to other primary solutions I proposed and delivered. So, it never ceased to amaze me that the job aid often seemed to be as or more effective in producing results than the primary solution. When I learned how to conduct return-on-investment analysis, I was stunned to see how the magnitude of the payoff with job aids compared to other options such as traditional classroom training or organization development interventions. I probably spent the first five years of my consulting career underestimating the impact of job aids on performance only to be reminded again and again about their potential effects on the bottom line. Conversations with frontline performers reinforced how valuable job aids can be.

Fortunately, I've learned from my early mistakes, and I've come to rely heavily on job aids, which are often the most effective and sensible approach to getting results for clients. These days, when internal and external consultants are pressured to generate results quickly with minimal resources, job aids are often the best approach to boost performance. Even if a job aid doesn't have the greatest impact on improving performance, sometimes it's the only realistic option in these time-pressured, resource-constrained times.

In short, job aids have never been more important.

Who Can Benefit From This Book?

This book is aimed at providing you the practical basics about job aids and their use and design. It was written specifically for people who have little or no experience in developing job aids, are just getting started in it, or need to find out more information about job aids. You'll find little emphasis on theory, models, or the pertinent literature in this book. The focus is on a practical understanding of the development and use of job aids. If you don't know much about job aids, this book is a very good place for you to start.

It's also important to make a point about the job aid examples presented in this book. I've tried to offer a range of examples including some from different consultants whose work I admire. In some cases, I provide general advice for formatting job aids, but not all of the job aid examples adhere strictly to some of that advice. The formatting rules aren't absolute, and I also wanted to show job aids from a range of different sources, including some very good consultants who have some different standards for formatting. Seeing different looks and styles to a range of job aids is an intentional strategy of this book, allowing you to compare them and form your own standards. Plus, it's also important to recognize that very few rules about job aids are absolute; a good designer knows when to break one rule in favor of another. One of the challenges in designing a job aid is that basic design rules (such as providing plenty of white space and explaining conditions for use) often come in conflict, making it necessary for the designer to have to determine which rule to break.

Icons to Guide You

This book has plenty to offer in the way of content that can help you every day. Some icons will alert you to key features of the book. Here are the ones you'll find throughout all of ASTD's *Training Basics* series:

What's Inside This Chapter

Each chapter opens with a short summary that serves as a quick reference to the chapter contents. Use this section to identify the information in the chapter and, if you wish, skip ahead to the material that is most useful to you.

Think About This

These are helpful tips that you can put in your back pocket to pull out when needed as you prepare to design a job aid.

Basic Rules

These rules cut to the chase. They are unequivocal and important concepts or rules of thumb.

Noted

This icon flags sections with greater detail or an explanation about a concept or a principle. Sometimes it is also used for a short but productive tangent.

Getting It Done

The final section of each chapter supports your ability to take the content of that chapter and apply it to your situation. The focus of this section is mostly on job aids and tools for understanding the content. Sometimes this section contains a list of questions for you to ponder, sometimes it is a self-assessment tool, and sometimes it is a list of action steps you can take to improve your skills and help increase the chances for participant success.

Acknowledgments

This book could not have been written without the support, advice, and wisdom of many people. Joe Harless was one of the first voices in the performance wilderness calling attention to the power of job aids. Allison Rossett is a giant on this topic, and her work has been a great resource; nearly every book, presentation, or paper on the subject draws upon her contributions. Tony Moore has some good resources online.

A host of consultants has entertained my foolish questions and shared their wisdom over the years while patiently explaining the error of my ways. I thank Paul Elliott, Joyce Kozuch, Michael Balbirer, Ethan Sanders, Mary Broad, George Piskurich, Geary Rummler, Dennis Mankin, Ken Kincaid, Janet Bernhards, Laurel Rosinger, Phil Anderson, Tim Griles, Cynthia Denton-Ade, Marcy Greenberg, David Mosher, and Rebecca Birch for insights that have contributed in various ways to this book. Many clients have allowed me to see their work and shared their insights and mistakes. All these folks have broadened my understanding of job aids and performance. Their contributions are reflected in the advice contained in this book

I also want to acknowledge a group of designers and performance consultants who allowed their work to be used in this book as examples. Specifically, I want to thank Cynthia Denton-Ade, Geary Rummler, William Wake, and Bill Horton. I acknowledge my son David for his support with graphics and production. As is true for many 11-year-olds of his generation, he's more computer literate than his parents are. Several of the job aid examples in this book are a result of his work.

Last of all, I wish to thank my wife, Cathy, for her support and encouragement throughout the entire process. Being married to a writer is no easy task but she has proven herself to be a saint.

Joe Willmore
March 2006

Why Focus on Job Aids?

What's Inside This Chapter

Here you'll find out:

▶ What a job aid is—and isn't
▶ Why job aids are so critical for trainers and performance consultants
▶ How to navigate this book and its structure to find specific information.

How *Job Aid Basics* Can Help You

You've probably heard the phrase "job aid" mentioned before. If you're a trainer or instructional designer or someone who provides support to performers, you probably have experience developing job aids. Or, maybe you've read some of the literature explaining how job aids are such an effective and cost-productive means of providing "just in time" performance support and it sounds like a good fit given the time-urgent client demands you face. You might have heard other people use the term "job aid," and you've decided you need to find out more about what job aids are and how to develop them. Perhaps you're trying to improve the ability of line managers and performers to develop quick, effective ways of dealing with some kinds of performance problems. Regardless of your reason, the act of picking up this book probably means you have some practical questions about job aids you'd like answered.

Well, the good news is that understanding job aids and learning how to design them isn't rocket science. This book was written with you in mind. It's an introduction to job aids so you'll know what they are and how they're used. Additionally, this book is a practical guide to designing and developing job aids. The material here focuses on delivering plenty of application advice, such as what type of job aid to use in particular situations and tips for designing specific job aids. Therefore, this book is full of job aid examples as well as activities to help you apply what you learn.

As you read the chapters, you'll start to notice a range of job aids in your world. In fact, you're surrounded by job aids. There are plenty of job aids—both well-designed and mistake-filled—that you encounter in the normal run of your daily life. Some of those job aids have been so integrated into people's everyday lives that most users fail to recognize them for what they are. That's fine; one sign of a good job aid is that it's accessible and easy to use when it's needed, yet invisible or unobtrusive when it's not. Part of your education about job aids can start by beginning to notice and evaluate these job aids that surround you in your daily life. Start by noticing some of these job aids—on kitchen appliances or in your car—and think about how helpful or confusing they are, what design elements work or get in the way, and the degree to which they support a particular task.

Why Use Job Aids?

Job aids are designed to provide information to support performers on specific job-related tasks. Joe Harless (1996), in his work with the Harless Performance Guild, found that the majority of performance problems could be attributed to information

Basic Rule 1

Job aids should be easily accessible yet unobtrusive. The purpose of a job aid is to support the performer. Therefore, the job aid should be easy to access and easy to use, but it shouldn't get in the way when it's not needed.

Noted

There are plenty of examples of job aids that appear to be elegant and well designed but are rarely used by the performers. In designing job aids, you should never lose sight of the performance context for the job aid. Job aids that look great or have superb detail may also be uncomfortable for performers to use if they don't want to appear ignorant to customers, or they might take too much time to access and utilize. You create a job aid to improve performance on a specific task. But, the performance improvement doesn't happen if the performers won't use the job aid you create. So, you need to understand the performers, the situation they work in, and what barriers exist to using a job aid. Consequently, accessibility, ease of use, and unobtrusiveness are critical for successful job aids.

issues. Job aids are designed to help address performance gaps due to information issues. Even though job aids address these problems, solutions that close performance gaps can have a large effect on the number of performance problems in a given organization. Therefore, because so many performance gaps are due to information issues, job aids are likely to be an appropriate solution for most organizations.

Additionally, job aids are often a very cost-effective solution (Harless, 1986) to many performance problems. In instances where an organization can choose from a range of possible interventions to deal with a problem, job aids often have the highest return-on-investment (ROI). This is because job aids typically don't involve the costs of such other options as training, conferences, or various kinds of information technology (IT) tools. The U.S. Coast Guard found that job aids can be developed 75 percent faster than training on a similar subject and that when job aids are available, the amount of time necessary for training is reduced substantially (2003). Job aids can usually be deployed much more quickly than organization-wide training. Even in instances where a job aid may not be as effective as another solution, on balance the job aid may still have a much higher ROI. Therefore, because of scarce resources and competition for your time, there will be many instances where a job aid will be the intervention of choice for a wide range of performance gaps.

Take the example of office equipment theft. If employees forget to lock outside doors when leaving for the day, some office supplies or equipment might be stolen from time to time because the building is not secure. The company could invest in

Basic Rule 2

Job aids typically have higher ROI percentages than other interventions. Because job aids typically minimize the amount of time performers need to be away from the job, even a job aid that only reduces (rather than eliminates) a performance gap usually generates ROI results that are much greater than competing interventions.

a series of security systems and automated doors that lock after closing time. This would likely eliminate the theft problem. A job aid, such as a sign by the door, reminding the last employee to leave for the day to lock the door would probably reduce the problem, but because the job aid won't be 100 percent effective (sometimes a person will forget to read the job aid or get distracted on the way out of the door), some theft will still occur. However, it's likely that the cost of the security and automation system would be so much greater than the cost of the job aid that even with some reduced level of theft (rather than complete elimination of the problem via automation), the job aid approach has a superior ROI.

Here's another way to evaluate the efficacy of job aids: Compare how a job aid can clarify and remind a performer on details that may prove difficult to remember. You can judge for yourself by looking at an example involving initial instructions and then a job aid that was developed when it became clear that the instructions weren't sufficient to eliminate performance problems. One client had problems with workers logging onto workstations to access a critical database. The problem that the client faced was twofold. First, the data on the workstations needed to remain confidential and secure so it was necessary to use a sign-on process to make sure that unintended users of the database were denied access. Second, because performers rarely needed to use that database, they tended to forget the login procedure. The result was wasted time, extra demands on the help desk, false alarms to system security, users' inability to access the database when needed, and at least three workstations that were damaged or destroyed beyond repair by frustrated users who failed in their attempts to sign on.

The organization attempted to deal with this problem by developing a set of instructions for signing onto the workstation. When the instructions failed to solve the problem, a job aid was developed. Compare the instructions (altered to protect security procedures for the organization in question) with the job aid that follows and judge for yourself the value of the job aid.

The text taken from the client instructional manual with instructions for signing onto a computer workstation basically reads as follows:

> All database workstations are secure and require multiple levels of user identity verification before the user can access the system or utilize the workstation. Prior to using the workstation, user authentication must take place. User identity must be verified by the user directly and individually by providing user work number, user-specific password and user name. For user name, users should be consistent with agency protocol. User number, user password and user name will have been assigned prior to utilizing the system and refer to the employee identification number, the individually determined password and the log-in name. The system log-on sequence will also ask the user to confirm his or her identity. This is done by typing in "yes" at the appropriate place in the sequence. The sequence in which the data is entered is critical for security approval. Nor is there a need to hit "enter" for each data query. Instead, this is necessary only at the conclusion of each screen. However, all queries must be complete. Failure to respond to any requested data will result in a denial of system access. Occasionally access will be denied. This is usually because of data entry errors by the user in the verification process. None of the data queries are case sensitive, but users must be sure that accurate replies are entered to each verification query. Should access be denied, users will be allowed one additional attempt to authenticate identity. Subsequent authentication attempts should not be attempted. Repeated failures at authentication will shut down the workstation and alert corporate security of a security violation with the database. Therefore, users who encounter two verification failure attempts should contact security at extension 3244 prior to proceeding further or attempting to log on. This is necessary to prevent workstation shutdown, authenticate user identity, and troubleshoot potential problems with the workstation user identity process. Although most errors are due to user error, there are occasionally system errors that are not due to user entry. In such cases, only corporate security is able to resolve such problems. Be sure to enter all data accurately to minimize authentication errors.

Here is the material from the instructional manual in the form of a job aid that was produced on a laminated sheet and attached to the side of the computer monitor:

1. When the system is on, a login screen will appear on the monitor.
2. Enter login name.

Think About This

Practically all training that either involves a significant delay before the new skills or knowledge is applied on the job or training for skills that are used infrequently would benefit greatly from a supporting job aid.

3. Enter password.
4. Hit "enter" on the keyboard.
5. When the corporate logo appears on the next screen, enter your employee identification number (the number on the front of your badge).
6. When the system asks you to confirm your name, type "yes."
7. You will be denied access after two failed attempts. Hit "enter" and you'll be granted access to the workstation. *Important:* If you are not initially granted access, you can repeat steps 2–7 in order one more time. Then you must contact corporate security at extension 3244. Do not try to log onto the workstation after two failed attempts.

Notice several key differences between the original instructional manual and the job aid. The original instructions indicate that the sequence of tasks is critical. For example, if the user doesn't enter the information in the correct order, then the computer won't allow the performer to log onto the system. However, this information is buried deep in the original instructions and would probably be missed by someone attempting to log on while simultaneously reviewing their instruction manual. In contrast, the job aid uses numbers to indicate clearly that the tasks are to be performed in a specific sequence, ensuring that users do not skip material or jump around. Additionally, the job aid provides the content in the sequence that the user will need the information (login name, password, and then employee identification number).

The original instructions are a mass of text that is difficult to read, especially when trying to perform another task, such as logging onto the computer workstation. The job aid offered plenty of white space and eliminated much of the text for clarity. White space is critical if the performer is likely to be switching eye contact from the job aid to a task or tool (in this case, the workstation screen).

Basic Rule 3

Less is more. As a rule of thumb, job aids benefit from less text and less explanation. That's because job aids are often meant to be used on the job while performing. More text or explanation is likely to interrupt the task and detract from performance, and might also discourage the performer from using the job aid.

Finally, the job aid was designed for just-in-time availability or multitasking. The content in the instructional manual would likely be forgotten by the time the user had to attempt to log onto the system because the training would have occurred months or even a year before the worker would ever need to use the database. The job aid was designed with the recognition that the person using the job aid probably would be attempting to sign on at the same time he or she was referring to the job aid. Therefore, the job aid allowed for quick eye capture of key points and sequence while it reduced the potential for confusion.

What's a Job Aid, Anyhow?

If you're new to job aids and don't have an extensive background in instructional design or performance consulting, you probably have only a vague sense of what people mean when they refer to a job aid. You probably know what the concept of a job aid is, but you might not be exactly clear what is and isn't a job aid. Let's take a look at what constitutes a job aid.

Job aids can take many forms, and they utilize a range of formats and media. Some examples of possible job aids are the following:

- ▶ a three-dimensional scale model or a replica
- ▶ a picture
- ▶ a checklist
- ▶ a manual or information guide
- ▶ a computer help screen or pull-down menu
- ▶ a to-do list
- ▶ presentation notes
- ▶ a buzzer or bell or alarm that goes off as a reminder of when to do something

▶ a troubleshooting guide

▶ software that shows the group meeting schedule.

Understanding Human Performance

Before defining what is and is not a job aid, it's valuable to get some perspective about human performance. Ethan Sanders and Sivasailam Thiagarajan (2002) developed a model for ASTD (based in part upon Thomas Gilbert's behavioral engineering approach) that breaks down the critical areas that are factors in human performance for identifying the cause of a performance gap and for determining what solutions to use to close that gap. According to their model, the six critical categories are:

1. *Structure/process:* This category includes company policies, reporting relationships, work sequence, work flow, job description, and organizational mission and vision. Structure/process deals with how the work and performers are organized.

2. *Resources:* This category includes tools, ranging from shovels to backhoes to computers and personal digital assistants (PDAs); sufficient staffing; appropriate funding amounts; and adequate amounts of time for the work assigned. Resource factors typically involve getting more of a particular work resource or improving the quality of the tool or resource.

3. *Information:* This category includes having clear direction about priorities, receiving feedback from customers, getting timely and accurate performance feedback, and being apprised about meetings or other relevant activities. It's important to note that information as a category is not about teaching the performer how to do a particular task. Rather, if information is the cause of the performance gap, that means the worker has the ability or skills to do the work but is missing some data or information that would allow the worker to use the appropriate skills to produce the desired result. For instance, you may know how to open a door, but the sign on the door informs you whether you should push out or pull in to open the door.

4. *Knowledge/skills:* This category includes providing various types of training, hiring smarter or more skilled performers, and redesigning tasks so they require less knowledge. Knowledge/skills addresses the basic issue of whether the performer has the ability to do the job.

5. *Motives:* This category includes worker burnout issues, incentives and benefits, unfair treatment or discrimination, and worker commitment to

organizational purpose. Motivation has to do with whether the performer wants to do the job well or if there are other factors that outweigh incentives to perform.

6. *Wellness:* This category includes work-related injuries, fatigue, mental illness, emotional trauma, and other factors that mean a performer is physically sub par. Wellness addresses whether the employee's health or variations in physical or emotional state could alter performance.

This six-part model is critical to understand job aids. Job aids aren't meant to close all types of performance gaps; rather, they are designed to provide information. Therefore, they can address only one of the six factors that affect performance. Now, it is true that a job aid could positively affect motivation. For example, if a worker receives a job aid, he or she might feel more confident and thus better motivated to take on challenging tasks. Or, a job aid might inadvertently provide a performer critical knowledge that enhances his or her ability to do the job. Even though it might affect motivation or build skills, that is not the initial intent behind the use of the job aid.

Job aids are designed to make information more readily available and useable for performers. This point is important because just as it's a mistake to throw training at problem that is not knowledge- or skill-related, it also is a mistake to use a job aid to address a problem that a job aid cannot solve. Therefore, one of the prerequisites to prescribing a job aid is to be sure that a job aid is the correct way to improve that performance problem. In the grand scheme of things, job aids are designed to address performance problems due to information issues. If customer service continually breaks down because the shipping process results in a failure to fill customer orders, creating a job aid will not fix the process and therefore won't solve the problem. However, it is important to note that if you do fix this problem (failure to fill customer orders) by changing the shipping process, you may need to create a job aid to inform and remind workers of the new process. Therefore, job aids will often be a critical support tool for a range of interventions. An organization may change resources (by upgrading computers), improve skills (by providing training), seek to motivate (by improving benefits) or enhance wellness (by providing a workout room); job aids may support any of these interventions (by providing details about how to use the computers effectively, reminders of the training content or new benefits, and details about the workout room use policy).

Noted

Performance gaps fall within six areas—structure/process, resources, information, knowledge/ skills, motivation, and wellness (Sanders & Thiagarajan, 2002). Job aids address only performance gaps attributable to information issues.

Think About This

Because job aids provide information or enhance memory, you'll probably find job aids to be effective support for other inventions you implement. For instance, you can use job aids to provide reminders and refreshers about training participants have taken or new policies and processes being implemented to improve performance. Therefore, job aids are often critical in supporting other types of interventions.

Jeannette Gautier-Downes and Allison Rossett (1991) have a widely accepted definition of what constitutes a job aid: It is "a repository for information, processes, or perspectives that is external to the individual and that supports work and activity by directing, guiding, and enlightening performance." Several key points of this definition are important to understand.

First, consider the term "repository." A job aid stores information for performers and than makes that information accessible or available. That's the primary purpose of a job aid. Now does a repository of information sound like a bookstore, library, or filing cabinet to you? Bookstores, libraries, and filing cabinets (even though they may be a place to find information) aren't job aids. People use the term "information" too loosely at times. Libraries, bookstores, or filing cabinets may have books or files that can teach how to do something (knowledge or skills). They do provide data on a wide range of subjects, but a job aid is designed with a specific task or performer in mind. Many things can be repositories of data but they are not necessarily job aids.

Second, think about the phrase "external to the individual." Performers are asked to remember all sorts of information that is critical to their job. That is where job aids come in. Sometimes the stress of the work situation makes it difficult to recall, or there may be so much information the performer must remember (or the worker rarely needs it so it's easily forgotten).

Third, the phrase "supports work" is what helps separate a job aid from something like a library. A job aid exists to support a specific task or performer, but it is not designed to teach or instruct. It is not a repository of data that various individuals may choose to use in any manner that benefits them.

Here is the definition of a job aid that this book uses: *A job aid is an external resource designed to support a performer in a specific task by providing information or compensating for lapses in worker memory.* How does this differ from the definition of Gautier-Downes and Rossett?

The term "specific task" indicates that a job aid is designed to help a performer with a particular piece of work or assignment. Absent this distinction (the focus on a specific task or piece of work), it becomes more difficult to distinguish between a job aid and general data sources that have no particular purpose other than to be useful. Also, "providing information or compensating for lapses in worker memory" emphasizes that it's important that job aids be used only for performance problems that are solvable by job aids. At the point that instruction or training takes place, it's not a job aid anymore. Job aids aren't designed to improve motivation or provide a better tool. Job aids address information issues.

These two distinctions ("specific task" and "providing information...") are important ones to make because they pertain to issues of design and evaluation. If you want to design an effective job aid, you need to be clear about its purpose and capabilities. Therefore, it is critical to target a specific task rather than look to produce something that is just a general resource of some kind without a particular performer or task in mind. Furthermore, the purpose of a job aid is to improve performance and thus obtain better results. So, it's important to emphasize providing information as a means of boosting performance. Finally, by emphasizing the "specific task" and "providing information...," this definition highlights two factors that are critical to distinguishing job aids from tools and instructional materials.

Some have referred to job aids as "performance support tools" or "task aids" (Long, 2004). There are many things that support performance or help people to do tasks. Practically any tool (from a bulldozer to a telescope to a wireless phone to a help

Noted

What distinguishes a job aid from other resources (such as a tool) is its purpose. A job aid's purpose is to be a repository for information on a specific task to improve performance.

desk) could be something that aids in a task or supports performance. Therefore, it's not sufficient to argue that something that helps a performer is a job aid. That would destroy the distinction between a job aid and a tool. The term "task aid" might be a better synonym for "job aid." In any case, it's important to note that other literature sometimes refers to job aids as performance support tools or task aids.

What Isn't a Job Aid?

You've seen information on what a job aid *is*. Now, let' take a quick look at what a job aid *isn't*. There is a tendency to confuse on the basis of format. For example, because many job aids may consist of a form (such as a checklist or a worksheet), it's easy to assume that anything that looks similar must also be a job aid. Remember that something isn't a job aid because of how it looks, it's a job aid because of its purpose. If it makes information accessible for a specific task, then it's a job aid. But, if it instructs someone by telling them how to do something they didn't know how to do, then it's a form of training and would be dealing with knowledge or skills. If the checklist doesn't exist to remind a worker what to do but instead is a document that must be filled out to meet job requirements, then it isn't a job aid but falls within structure/process (as a work requirement to prove someone did the work). Something that helps someone to do work better isn't necessarily a job aid. Providing employees with laptop computers to take on the road might improve performance but this intervention (a laptop for each employee) is a tool, not a job aid. There are plenty of tools and resources that help performers do better work, but those same tools and resources don't necessarily qualify as job aids. If it isn't about providing information or aiding recall specific to a task, then it isn't a job aid.

What's the Difference Between a Job Aid and a Tool?

It's easy to confuse job aids and tools initially. The distinguishing characteristic between the two involves their purposes or functions or uses. A job aid is a repository for information. It may have the effect of enhancing performance by improving user confidence. For example, an experienced speaker might have notes on index cards. The mere presence of the cards might boost the speaker's confidence, but the purpose of the job aid (the presentation notes on the index cards) is to reduce what the speaker needs to remember. It is an unintended consequence that the job aid improves confidence and, thus, performance. The primary purpose of a job aid is to hold information so the performer doesn't need to remember it.

A tool enables a performer to do something that would otherwise be undoable. Examples would be a wrench used to tighten a nut or a parachute that allows someone to jump out of a flying airplane and survive the landing. Even if the performer could do the task without the tool, the tool allows the worker to do the work faster, easier, or better by increasing precision or consistency. A tool doesn't exist primarily to provide information or compensate for memory—that's the description of a job aid. A tool might assist someone with a task, or a tool could even complete it for the worker (such as software that checks for viruses on a computer without any involvement of the worker other than initially configuring the software to conduct the viral scan automatically at a set time).

Is an EPSS a Job Aid?

EPSS stands for electronic performance support system. An EPSS is capable of being either a job aid or a tool. Some examples of EPSSs that are also a job aids are

▶ a file containing a list of phone numbers and addresses (so performers don't have to remember all of this data)
▶ an electronic calendar or scheduler that retains meeting and commitments (so staff members don't forget when meetings are scheduled)
▶ a pull-down menu within a software program that reminds a user the correct keystrokes for particular hypertext mark-up language (HTML) codes.

The key element in all these examples is that the performer already knows how to do the work, but the EPSS aids in memory or provides information. In none of these cases is the EPSS providing a skill that the performer does not already have.

An EPSS can also be a tool and, therefore, not a job aid. For instance, an EPSS can be a global positioning system (GPS) device that identifies exactly where the user is located by tapping into GPS satellite signals. An EPSS can also be software that automatically restructures a document to fit new formatting requirements or performs a word count or analyzes the sentence structure for grammatical errors. In all of these cases, even if the performer had the ability to do this work without the EPSS, it serves as a tool either by doing the work for the performer (thus automating the work) or by allowing the work to be faster or more efficient. However, in these examples the EPSS does not compensate for lapses in worker memory. The spell-checking software is faster than a visual check by the performer not because of human memory but because the software tool can review the entire document faster than the human can read it and is thus more efficient.

Therefore, EPSS could be a job aid or a tool. It is accurate to say that in the world of possible job aids and the world of possible EPSSs, there is some overlap between the two. But, not all job aids are EPSSs and not all EPSSs are job aids. The key is to discern the purpose: If the purpose is to provide information or aid memory, then it's a job aid. If the purpose is anything else, then it's a tool.

Getting It Done

Now that you've had an opportunity to get some sense of what a job aid is and the potential value a job aid can provide, exercise 1-1 provides some additional things you can do that will position you for the rest of the book and allow you to apply what you have learned thus far.

Exercise 1-1. Getting started with job aids.

1. Identify at least three examples of job aids that you use in your life. They can be personal or professional uses. If your initial reaction is that you don't use any job aids, try looking in your kitchen or the dashboard of your car and you'll find a range of job aid examples to choose from. What did you like about each job aid? In what ways were they cumbersome or poorly designed? To what extent did you need to interrupt or stop performing a task to use the job aid?

2. Identify at least three examples from your work where a job aid would be helpful but is not currently available. Specifically, think of tasks that require you to use your memory or instances where you tend to forget important information that is necessary to complete the job.

3. Identify at least one instance at work where a job aid might have been a cheaper or more effective alternative to an intervention (such as training, an organization development activity, job restructuring, changing of job duties, or automation) that was used to address a performance problem. Why would the job aid have been more effective or less expensive?

Answering these questions can help you to find some job aid samples from your own life as well as possible opportunities. Later in this book, you'll get an opportunity to practice developing your own job aids. A good way to start is to begin by finding opportunities with your own work that right now would benefit from a job aid; that way you'll be doing something that has immediate application, you have some background about it, and you'll be able to see a practical return. The next chapter looks at different types of job aids and identifies what circumstances benefit from job aids.

2

Vive la Différence: Understanding Job Aid Format Choices

What's Inside This Chapter

Here you'll find out:

▶ Types of or formats for job aids
▶ Examples of each job aid format
▶ Advice on choosing one job aid format over another.

In chapter 1 you learned what a job aid is, but there is more than just one type of job aid because performers have different types of informational needs. Additionally, not all informational needs are well suited for job aids. Although job aids come in many types of formats, lengths, and media, you need to determine if the work setting and performer background are appropriate for a job aid (or if some other kind of solution is more appropriate).

The purpose behind a job aid is to provide data or information so that a performer can minimize the need to memorize task details while applying existing skills and knowledge. That's a basic description of what job aids do. However, there are many different types of performers, work situations, tasks, and information needs.

Consequently, there are many different types or formats for job aids. One way to distinguish among the various job aid formats is by how the information is conveyed by each job aid or the specific purpose of the job aid. For instance, some job aids seek to standardize performance, others provide a starting and ending point, still others provide the "big picture" or context for the work, and so on.

The 10 Job Aid Formats

Depending upon the source, there are a range of different types or formats for job aids. Long (2004) refers to four formats. Others (Gautier-Downes & Rossett, 1991) refer to seven formats. This book distinguishes 10 different job aid formats, which are described in greater detail in the sections that follow:

- ▶ reminder
- ▶ match
- ▶ step
- ▶ checklist
- ▶ worksheet
- ▶ process table or flowchart
- ▶ decision table
- ▶ troubleshooting diagram
- ▶ data array
- ▶ script.

 Noted

It's useful to differentiate the different job aid formats because each format has different design considerations and fits different performance issues. If you identify the performance challenges first, then it is easier to determine which job aid format would be the best.

Reminder

This is typically the simplest, most basic form of job aid. The Reminder job aid prompts performer behavior with a simple set of instructions. Often these instructions consist of a single sentence or phrase. The information provided in this format isn't structured, doesn't involve a range of data or involve any sequence. It can consist of a decal taped to a telephone with the phone number for poison control or a reminder inscribed on a tire next to the air valve listing the PSI (pounds per square inch) pressure for the tire. One classic example of such a job aid is the U.S. military claymore antipersonnel mine. To ensure that inexperienced soldiers or troops under fire don't panic and point the claymore in the wrong direction, the face of the weapon bears the inscribed text "Front Toward Enemy," so that even in darkness, mud, or confusing circumstances the solder deploying it can place it properly, facing away from friendly forces (figure 2-1).

Figure 2-1. Claymore antipersonnel mine: example of a job aid integrated into a tool.

Noted

A Reminder job aid tends to be simpler than many of the other formats. It doesn't have a sequence or order, depict a process, or involve a checklist or any type of decision tree to work through.

What is typically the major challenge for the Reminder job aid is usability. All job aids need to be easily accessible and easy to use. Almost all job aids typically serve as reminders of one sort or another. But, the Reminder job aid must be able to provide the information in the work environment so that it's easy for the performer to access it without stopping or slowing down. The Reminder format is typically used in instances where the designer wants to avoid interrupting the task or is aware that the nature of the work environment won't allow for much time (if any) to consult a reference. In other words, Reminder job aids are rarely ones where a performer can step away from the work to read a sheet of paper, consult a manual, or refer to a detailed help screen. Thus, many Reminder job aids are instances where the information is integrated into a tool or it becomes part of the product. An example of this type of job aid is when people write down their password or personal identification number so they can sign onto a computer or access a bank account at an automatic teller.

Reminder job aids are often improvised on the spot and, although rough, can be very effective. During the Apollo 13 space mission, pilot Jack Swigert resorted to just such a job aid. As the three astronauts worked desperately to stay alive and keep their damaged space craft functioning despite a host of obstacles, Swigert was afraid that in his sleep- and oxygen-deprived condition he might accidentally push the jettison switch (which would cause part of the Apollo spacecraft to separate from the lunar module drifting off into space with crew members Fred Haise and Mission Commander Jim Lovell still on board). To prevent this from happening, Swigert took a piece of paper torn from a manual, wrote "NO" on it and used duct tape to cover the LEM JETT (jettison) switch (Lovell & Kluger, 1994).

Think About This

Oftentimes you can identify needs for job aids by examining improvised versions that workers have developed on their own. For instance, when you see a handwritten card taped to the dashboard of a truck that says "Check tire pressure before leaving station," that should give you a hint that this improvised Reminder job aid might be better served by something with more planning (such as a checklist next to the truck cab listing items to go over before leaving with the delivery). As a training developer and job aid designer, it's often useful to visit the worksite and see what performers have done to remind themselves of what they need to do. Also, exemplary performers often generate their own impromptu job aids (often in the Reminder format), so finding out what the key performers have done is often a good indicator.

Match

This type of job aid provides an example or model for the worker to compare work against. It shows the performer what the final product is supposed to look like. It can also be an alignment or quality specification resource by demonstrating what the product needs to match or be identical to. Typically this format allows for comparison between the job aid example and the finished product. For instance, because of concerns about falsification of identity documents, many organizations post a job aid for clerks at checkout counters to show an example of a legitimate driver's license so they can compare a customer's license with the picture of what a genuine license looks like (figure 2-2).

Figure 2-2. Example of the Match job aid format.

A picture of this sample identification card for minors would be disseminated to people (such as liquor store proprietors, retail clerks that sell cigarettes, or movie theater cashiers) so they could compare the identity cards of customers with the Match example and thus spot fraudulent cards.

A Match job aid may also consist of a model or replica so that the performer can compare the finished product to the job aid as a reminder of what the work should look like. A Match job aid usually doesn't focus on how the work is done; rather, it provides an example of what the result is supposed to look like. The performer thus can tell if the work is correct or acceptable by how closely it matches the example provided in the job aid. Examples of this job aid include pictures used in restaurants to remind staff members how the food on a plate is to be arranged or a diagram that shows a mechanic the correct placement of a registration decal (figure 2-3).

Figure 2-3. Another example of a Match job aid.

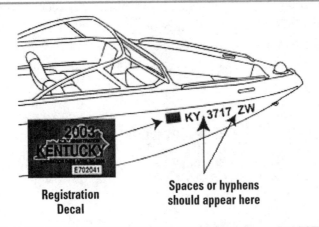

Three-dimensional models or samples can be excellent Match job aids. These models serve as baselines or quality measures to guide what the final work product should resemble. Think of a potter or ceramic artist attempting to make a set of bowls of a similar size, shape, circumference, and depth. Even though there are tools (such as calipers) that a potter could use to make sure the bowls are close in size, there would need to be an initial starting point to shoot for with the bowls. The potter is likely to produce one bowl and then use it as a comparison for subsequent efforts, attempting to have the following bowls match the first one. In this instance, the first bowl (being used for comparison) is a Match job aid and serves as the model that all other bowls should match.

Another version of such a job aid would be a sample or prototype that a worker could use as a guide to copy from. In this instance, the purpose would not be to duplicate the example, only to use the Match job aid to develop something roughly similar. Sample form letters (figure 2-4) are a good example of this version of the Match job aid. This type of format is often good if there is no need to specify the process or sequence of the work because there is lots of variability or the performer is given discretion in what path to choose. This is also a good format if the work is new and the performer is uncertain or inexperienced at judging the quality of the finished product.

Figure 2-4. A sample notification letter: example of a Match job aid.

Sample Notification Letter
(Print on agency letterhead)

June 20, 2000

Mr. and Mrs. James Hillwood
1923 Dunster Lane
Arlington, VA 22009

Dear Mr. and Mrs. Hillwood:

On June 14, 2000, the Governor declared Arlington a disaster area due to the recent flooding of the Potomac River. Our community has been approved for grant money under the Hazard Mitigation Grant Program, or HMGP. Under this program, which is administered by the State Emergency Management Agency, we can acquire properties damaged by the flood. Those property owners who decide to sell their properties to the City can then relocate to less hazardous areas outside the floodplain. The City will only acquire property from property owners who voluntarily choose to sell their properties. The City of Arlington will *not* use its power of eminent domain to acquire property.

To be eligible for acquisition, properties must meet the following criteria:

- Have a substantially damaged structure(s) because of the June 2000 flooding of the Potomac River. "Substantially damaged" means the cost of restoring the structure to its pre-disaster condition would be equal to or more than 50 percent of its pre-disaster market value. Substantially damaged structures must be inspected and certified by the county building inspector.
- Include a primary residence or place of business.
- Be located in a floodplain that has flooded at least three times since January 1977.

According to our records, your property might meet these criteria. If you are interested in learning more about Property Acquisition under the HMGP, please attend one of the informational meetings listed below.

Grosvenor High School	National Guard Armory	Lee Community Center
2929 Tang Avenue	13 Wilson Blvd	3941 Talon Way
7:30 p.m.	10:00 a.m.	11:00 a.m. or 4:00 p.m.
Tuesday, June 26, 2000	Thursday, June 28, 2000	Saturday, June 30, 2000

If you have any questions, please call (222) 222-2222. Thank you.

Sincerely,

Marla Mason
Deputy Director, Arlington Emergency Management Agency

Think About This

People have a range of preferred learning styles (visual, kinetic, auditory, and so forth). Match job aids can be a particularly effective means for performers who are visual or kinetic learners. You can produce a replica or model they can touch or see to compare to the work they're producing.

Step

A Step job aid focuses on the sequence or correct order of a job. Typically, a Step job aid is used when it makes sense to break the work down into steps (usually because of complexity of the task or because the order of the steps is critical for success). Usually a Step job aid is used for a performer who does the work from start to finish or needs to be sure the actions are performed in the correct sequence. A Step job aid is especially invaluable when the task involves actions that cannot be reversed or reordered if the result is to be successful. For example, recipes are examples where the sequence matters greatly (figure 2-5). Imagine a cake where some of the ingredients are put in the pan, baked, only then are the ingredients mixed and the eggs and sugar added. That is not likely to be a cake you'd want to eat!

A Step job aid is more than just a diagram of the process or flow of the work. Depicting the process is appropriate for someone who is trying to understand how the tasks integrate together. A performer might examine the process halfway through the work to get a better understanding of the "big picture." A Step job aid, however, is designed for someone who is either starting at the beginning of the process with jobs where task sequence matters or when it is easy for the performer to get the work tasks out of order. Consequently, one of the defining elements for this type of job aid is that there is one path with a definable start and end. Another clue is that most (but not all) Step job aids have numbers to indicate the correct order or sequence.

Checklist

This job aid serves as a reminder of the items to be completed or inspected. A Checklist job aid often calls for the performer to actually check off work to indicate that it is completed. Typically Checklist and Step job aids differ in several aspects.

Figure 2-5. Example of the Step job aid format.

Chocolate-Caramel Cheesecake Recipe

Ingredients: (Crust) 1 package (8.5 ounces) of Nabisco Famous Wafers finely ground up (or their equivalent in Oreo cookies), 2 tablespoons sugar, 1/3 cup melted butter, pinch of salt.

1. Combine crumbs, sugar, butter and salt—mix well.
2. Press mixture firmly into the sides and bottom of a 10-inch springform pan.
3. Chill for 30 minutes (so butter can harden).

Ingredients: (Filling) 12 ounces of sweet chocolate (ideally milk chocolate), 2 pounds of cream cheese (four 8-ounce packages) at room temperature, 1 cup sugar, three eggs (or equivalent egg substitute), 1 teaspoon vanilla, 1/3 cup caramel sauce or melted caramels.

1. Preheat oven to 350 degrees F.
2. Melt chocolate so it is soup-like.
3. In a mixer, beat cream cheese with sugar until fluffy.
4. Add eggs to cream cheese/sugar mixture and beat.
5. Add vanilla and chocolate to mixture and beat.
6. Pour mixture into springform pan.
7. Pour caramel sauce on top of mixture in pan. Take a butter knife or spatula and use it to swirl or twist through the mixture (being careful not to hit the crust). The purpose is to disperse the caramel sauce through the cream cheese mixture without completely stirring it in.
8. Place springform pan in oven on middle rack and bake approximately 45 to 50 minutes. During baking, the top will rise and then collapse.
9. Remove from oven, cool, and then serve.

Source: Reprinted with permission from Joe Willmore. 2005.

Think About This

A Step job aid is designed either for someone to use while performing (so the worker can refer to it while doing the task) or so it's easy enough to retain—referring to it before starting the task. In either case, this means it's critical for a Step job aid to have plenty of white space (so the performer's eyes don't get lost in text) and the format be straightforward—either easy to retain or easy to follow while multitasking.

With a Step job aid, the sequence of the work is critical. With a Checklist, the sequence often doesn't matter; what's critical is that all items on the list are checked off. A Step job aid is a reminder of how to do the work by showing the performer how to get from the beginning to the end. A Checklist job aid more typically shows the result—what must be reviewed for the job to be done.

Checklist job aids are often helpful as quality control tools. Another way that Checklist job aids can have a multiple purpose is for supervisory oversight. If the manager can't be there to ensure the worker covers all of the bases, the manager can review the completed Checklist after work. To-do lists (offering a reminder of what needs to be done) or grocery lists (indicating what items need to be purchased) are good Checklist examples. Figure 2-6 offers an example of a Checklist job aid.

Figure 2-6. Example of the Checklist job aid format.

Is my password secure?

> Could someone learn your password and use it to obtain classified information from our systems? Take this simple self-audit to see how secure your password really is.
>
> ☐ Is your password just letters or just numbers?
>
> ☐ Is it shorter than eight characters?
>
> ☐ Is it made of a single common word?
>
> ☐ Is it based on your birthday or that of a spouse or child?
>
> ☐ Is it based on your Social Security number or driver's license number?
>
> ☐ Is it based on the name of a child, spouse, or close relative?
>
> ☐ Have you had the same password for more than 2 months?
>
> ☐ Is your password written down somewhere and not under lock and key?
>
> If you answered yes to any of these questions, you are a security risk. Change your password **now.**

Source: Reprinted with permission from William Horton Consulting. 1999.

Although Checklist job aids don't necessarily require a sequence, good design takes into account whether a particular intuitive order makes sense with the items involved. Additionally, some tasks not only require a Checklist, but also involve a sequence. For instance, a pilot of a single-engine prop plane going through a pre-flight check would do a visual walk-around of the aircraft (to examine flaps and ailerons) before entering the cockpit and checking instruments. Then, once the plane has power, the pilot checks the oil pressure and gauge readings. The pilot can't check oil pressure until the propeller is turning. Therefore, the Checklist job aid to ensure all critical items are checked would also involve a sequence in this case.

Worksheet

This type of job aid provides a format, usually for some type of calculation, for performers to work on. Worksheets typically help keep the work neater or remind the performer of the format for the calculations and thus minimize errors caused by sloppiness. Tax forms are good examples of Worksheet job aids (figure 2-7).

Figure 2-7. Example of the Worksheet job aid format.

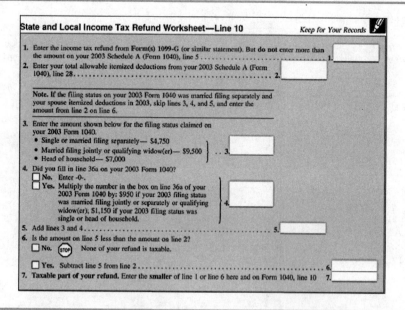

Worksheet job aids often imply a sequence although it may not be explicit. There is typically only one path (rather than multiple options) or one approach to complete the material. The performer usually fills in the blanks. Thus, the Worksheet job aid can be a useful method for also dealing with performer sloppiness. It is also a good approach for dealing with work involving numbers or calculations. By providing some of the content and format, the job aid can keep the work in the margins or provide sufficient space to reduce clerical errors.

A Worksheet job aid can be an effective means of getting performers to do particular kinds of work using the same method or process. For example, look at how customers document product problems when preparing to return a defective item. There may be multiple ways for customers to document problems with a product (and you can't dictate how they report the data), but you'd like to encourage uniformity in reporting to make it easier to process return requests as well as compile data for analysis. A Worksheet job aid (figure 2-8) would encourage customers to use the method outlined provided in the materials.

Figure 2-8. Another example of the Worksheet job aid format.

Customer Returns Calculation

Use this worksheet for each individual customer return (a return can include multiple products as long as they were purchased by the same customer on the same date and the same purchase order or check).

Initial day of product delivery	Day of product return	A. Total number of business days between product delivery and product return
Price per product (minus taxes and handling charges)	Number of products purchases	B. Total product purchase amount (price per product × number of products)
Total handling and delivery charges to customer (does not include taxes)	Total costs to customer to return defective products (Please include documentation of costs)	C. Difference between handling/delivery costs and total return costs
		D. Total repair costs by customer spent on defective products prior to return (Please include documentation of costs)
		Please add boxes B, C, and D and list total amount here

Process Table or Flowchart

This job aid format shows how a series of actions connect to form a process. Thus, a Process Table or Flowchart job aid identifies the work process (figure 2-9). Most job aids focus on a particular task. Examples include the correct process for transferring a call, legal and illegal questions to ask in an interview, or a chart to help diagnose why a computer keeps crashing. But, a Process Table or Flowchart job aid often deals with more than one particular task; this type of job aid frequently involves tasks that are integrated or related to each other.

A Process Table or Flowchart is similar to a Step job aid in that it shows the sequence for performing the work. Typically, however, a Step job aid is designed to guide a worker through the task from start to finish.

A Process Table or Flowchart typically serves two informational purposes. First, it can be used to provide an overall view of work—the "big picture" that the performer's task fits within. Although a Step job aid might show the sequence involved in producing a particular product or completing a particular task, a Process Table might be used to show larger and more involved sequences (such as how an organization shares information or the production process). Second, a Process Table or Flowchart is also useful if there is no natural starting point. Instead, the performer might be called to intervene at any stage of the process. This is especially true for processes that are circular and involve feedback loops.

Think About This

A Process Table or Flowchart job aid is often useful for customer care associates who need to answer particular customer questions. For instance, you may be responsible for receiving and recording customer complaints about recently purchased computers. But, if an upset customer wants to do more than record a complaint—if he or she wants to know what office is responsible for approving replacement of the computer or when to expect a refund—you need to know answers to issues outside of your responsibility. Having a Flowchart that identifies how the complaint process works would be invaluable for a performer whose job involves recording customer problems.

Figure 2-9. Example of a Flowchart job aid.

Customer Appeal Process

Customer product redemption follows this process to maintain record accuracy.

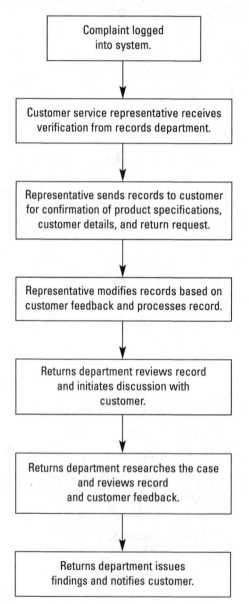

Decision Table

A Decision Table job aid displays information for performers and helps them sort through the various options to reach a decision or make an evaluation. This type of job aid helps performers distinguish among various options and pick the right course of action. A Decision Table job aid may also help workers discriminate between data. For instance, given a range of difference pieces of data, a Decision Table job aid helps the performer identify which data is critical and how to distinguish between different variables. The example in figure 2-10 was developed for the U.S. Navy Criminal Investigation Service to help investigators distinguish different types of gunshot wounds. You'll notice how the job aid points out critical distinguishing factors and helps the performer use those factors to identify what type of gunshot wound the agent is looking at.

A Decision Table is especially helpful for reminding the worker what factors to consider, what criteria to apply, or what elements are associated with particular issues. An example of a Decision Table job aid would be a tax table that identifies the exemptions a citizen is eligible for, depending upon his or her income and filing status. Unlike a Step job aid, a Decision Table can usually be entered at multiple points; there is not a fixed start or stop point. A Decision Table format can be very effective to enhance the judgment of new performers or help clarify critical factors for decisions.

Think About This

A Decision Table job aid is especially effective with complex tasks that involve a great deal of data because the Decision Table can highlight the data that is critical for the performer to consider. This does not mean that the Decision Table is effective for providing information on a task that might involve many possible outcomes, only that the Decision Table serves to simplify a complex series of factors. The Decision Table is also especially useful for new performers. Even though the stated purpose is to provide information, the Decision Table is one kind of job aid that can provide confidence to a new performer who can fall back on the job aid if there is a crisis of confidence.

Figure 2-10. Example of the Decision Table job aid format

Deaths Involving Firearms			
If the wound looks...	***And* you see...**	***And* there is...**	**Then it could be this type of wound...**
Round	A reddish-brown ring of abrasion	Minimal bleeding	Exit wound
		"Tattooing" in the skin around the wound	Close contact
Large, ragged	Star-like patterns	⟶	Contact over hard surface
	Separate overlapping perforations ("cookie cutter" effect)	⟶	Close contact shotgun wound
Ragged, irregular	A wound larger than the bullet	Maximum bleeding with protruding internal tissue	Exit wound
Ragged, with torn skin and tissue radiating from the hole	Unburned or partially burned gunpowder below the surface	⟶	Close contact over soft tissue
Diffused	No central hole	⟶	Distance shotgun wound

This job aid would be used by officers of the Navy Criminal Investigation Service to analyze the nature of a gunshot wound.

Source: Created by Cynthia Denton-Ade for the U.S. Navy Criminal Investigation Service.

Troubleshooting Diagram

A Troubleshooting Diagram helps a performer systematically identify problems or answers to problems. Typically, this job aid consists of a series of decision tables that follow a sequence or process to help a performer narrow down the definition of a problem or determine the cause of a problem. A good example of a Troubleshooting Diagram job aid is the kind of material often provided in auto repair manuals or car owner's manuals to allow someone to systematically rule out causes for malfunctions until the correct problem is identified. One of the distinctions between a Decision Table and a Troubleshooting Diagram is that a Decision Table involves choosing from a number of options to determine the correct answer. In contrast, a Troubleshooting Diagram consists of a series of decision diagrams at several levels; each decision takes the performer to another decision and then another, depending upon the complexity of the problem. The Troubleshooting Diagram also involves a process or sequence for analyzing the information (figure 2-11).

Good Troubleshooting Diagram job aids often are very complex. For instance, many machine repair guides utilize such approaches. Decision Tables seek to take complex data and simplify it by pointing out the critical variables to focus on and showing how to distinguish among cases or factors. In contrast, Troubleshooting Diagrams seek to be systematic and usually involve a sequence. An effective Troubleshooting Diagram rules out factors and verifies information and follows an analytical process. Consequently, Decision Tables and Troubleshooting Diagrams might sound similar at first, but they approach a performer problem ("What should I do? What is it?") through different means.

Data Array

Oftentimes a performer has a body of data that is necessary for the job. In such instances, a Data Array job aid can display the information so that the performer can pick out the relevant information. A typical example would be a list of postal zip codes that a worker needs to consult when calling clients or mailing out correspondence. Such information would be difficult to remember without the job aid.

The Data Array does not offer guidance on which information to choose, so it isn't a Decision Table or Troubleshooting Diagram. There is no sequence to it so it isn't a Step or Process Table job aid. Also, the performer isn't likely to need all of the data at the same time. For instance, the information in this job aid could be a list of phone numbers, and the performer would pull out the appropriate number as needed. The Data Array is simply a body of information that the performer is likely to need but no longer must memorize, thanks to the job aid (figure 2-12).

Script

This type of job aid provides text that a performer is either supposed to follow or may fall back on when dealing with customers. In some cases, the worker is expected to memorize the script and the job aid is simply there as either as a contingency or to build confidence in the performer. If memory fails, the performer can fall back on the

Figure 2-11. Example of the Troubleshooting Diagram job aid format.

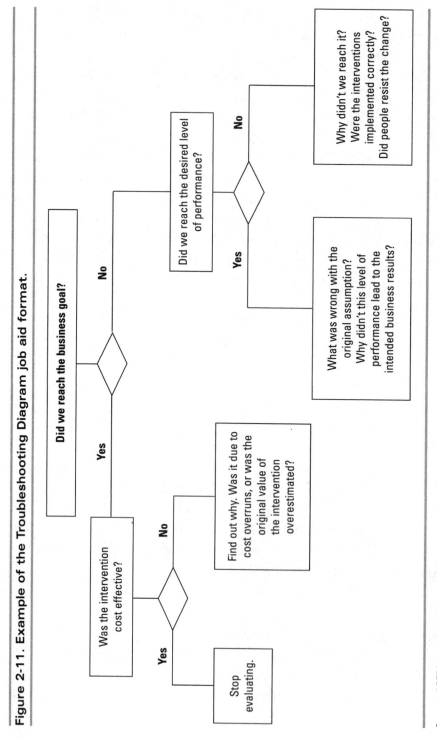

Did we reach the business goal?

No

Yes

Was the intervention cost effective?

No

Yes

Stop evaluating.

Find out why. Was it due to cost overruns, or was the original value of the intervention overestimated?

Did we reach the desired level of performance?

No

Yes

Why didn't we reach it?
Were the interventions implemented correctly?
Did people resist the change?

What was wrong with the original assumption?
Why didn't this level of performance lead to the intended business results?

Source: ASTD's approach to summative analysis. Based on the "HPI in the Workplace" course. Unpublished. Printed with permission from ASTD, Alexandria, VA.

Figure 2-12. Example of the Data Array job aid format.

Mid-Atlantic ASTD Chapter Websites	
Blue Ridge (Charlottesville)	www.blueridgeastd.org
Greater Richmond	www.rastd.org/
Maryland	www.astdmaryland.org
Metro DC Chapter (Washington, DC)	www.dcastd.org/
Southeastern Virginia (Hampton Roads)	www.sevaastd.org/
Valleys of Virginia (Roanoke)	www.roanokeastd.com/

Think About This

It's easy to make the mistake of creating a Data Array job aid that contains so much information that it ceases to be usable for the performer. Effective Data Array job aids often start by identifying what information the performer is most likely to have to access frequently. Instead of listing all possible options on a Data Array job aid, focus on the most frequently asked questions (FAQs) or the most common phone numbers requested by customers.

Script job aid. Sometimes, the Script job aid recognizes that the verbal content is too much for the worker to memorize or that the content changes too frequently to expect someone to always have it memorized. Scripts are also useful when precision of the wording is so critical that the performer is expected to say exactly those words and not deviate from the language.

The Script job aid does not provide a process or sequence in the sense that there are no clearly delineated steps. With some versions of the format, the words for the performer consist of only one or two sentences. For some Script job aids, the performer may read what is on the job aid word for word, the order of much of the content might not matter; what is critical is that the particular sentences be delivered accurately even if the sequence varies.

A classic example of a Script job aid is the Miranda warning that police in the United States are expected to deliver to individuals who've just been arrested. To be absolutely sure that the warning is delivered completely (and thus eliminate one grounds for dismissal of charges), many arresting officers carry the Miranda warning on a pocket card job aid (figure 2-13) to ensure that the arresting officer completely informs suspects about their rights. Other examples of Script job aids involve the canned dialog written for telemarketers as they pitch products or the official greeting that some companies expect receptionists to provide when answering an incoming call.

Figure 2-13. Example of the Script job aid format.

> ## MIRANDA RIGHTS
>
> "You are under arrest for your part in the offense of
>
> _____.
>
> I hereby notify you that you have a right to remain silent and you are not required to make any statement unless you want to do so voluntarily. Anything you say will be used against you in a court of law. You also have a right to consult with your attorney and have him present with you. If you cannot afford an attorney, one will be appointed to represent you."

Think About This

Script job aids can be very useful if it's important that the performer not deviate from the text at all. Such job aids are also useful as a "crutch" and confidence builder for new performers who know that if they forget something they can fall back on the Script. Just knowing that the job aid is there boosts the performers' confidence sufficiently so that they don't need it!

Combinations

One could argue for an 11th job aid format—the Combination. Plenty of job aids don't rely on a single format. Instead, the job aid may be both a Step and a Decision Tree format used together. The idea of combining formats makes sense for many performance issues. For instance, you'll probably see a number of customer service job aids that involve Troubleshooting Diagrams with Scripts so that the customer service representative knows what to say as he or she figures out what the problem is. Although this book doesn't count the Combination as a separate format, it's important to recognize that job aids often come in hybrid form. Once you begin designing job aids and try to identify which format is appropriate for the task, you'll probably discover that an approach that combines two or more formats is often the best method.

Getting It Done

Now that you've had a look at the different job aid formats and some specific examples of each of those formats for various tasks, exercise 2-1 has some activities for you to practice applying what you've learned.

Exercise 2-1. Thinking about job aids you use.

1. Think back to the "Getting It Done" work you did at the end of chapter 1. One assignment was to identify three job aids you currently use in your life. Looking at those three job aids, what format does each one fall into?

2. Which of the 10 job aid formats do you use the most and why? Which do you use the least and why?

3. Think back to the "Getting It Done" work you did at the end of chapter 1. One assignment was to identify at least three performance issues at work that might benefit from job aids. Choose one of those performance gaps and try to identify which of the 10 job aid formats might be a good fit for that problem.

(continued on page 38)

4. Do a quick review of the job aid examples provided in this chapter to illustrate each type of job aid format. Of the multiple examples provided, which one seemed to you to be the best designed? Considering the nature of the task, the type of performer, the format of the job aid, the decisions about what content to conclude or exclude, the media used—which job aid seemed to be a particularly good fit? Was there a particular example that seemed to be less helpful or appropriate from your perspective?

It's quite understandable if you found some of the questions in the exercise a bit challenging. After all, the book hasn't yet covered the principles of good design or the development process. But, you're being asked these questions to get you thinking about these issues and to identify your initial reactions to these issues. Then when you get to chapter 3 and subsequent sections of the book that go into detail about design and development of job aids, you can compare your initial reactions to your insights after a more detailed analysis and critique.

3

Determining Appropriate
Job Aid Use

▪▪

What's Inside This Chapter

Here you'll find out:

▶ When job aids might be a good fit
▶ How to pick the appropriate job aid format
▶ When to bundle a job aid with other interventions versus a
  stand-alone initiative
▶ Issues to consider with technology and job aid options.

Now that you're aware of the different types of job aids, it becomes critical to make wise decisions about when a job aid is appropriate and how to choose the right format. Each job aid format is appropriate for dealing with particular performance challenges; therefore, you need to choose the format that fits the needs of the performer and challenges of the work situation. This chapter can help you with those decisions.

Not Always

You'd think that in a book about job aids and how to use them, that you'd see claims about how they're so effective they can do all but cure cancer as well as fit nearly every performance situation. The reality is somewhat different. Job aids can be nearly miraculous in terms of their impact on performance and are usually very cost-effective approaches to dealing with work problems. But, as the first chapter noted, job aids don't deal with all kinds of performance problems. As you probably recall from the first chapter, job aids are effective only for information and memory issues. Consequently, you don't want to use a job aid to address a performance gap that deals with motivation or organizational structure or resources. Additionally, it doesn't make sense to add job aids without a good rationale for their use—job aids can contribute to performance problems if they distract the performers, force workers to halt the tasks to refer to them, or if they get in the way. The key to job aid success is appropriateness—the right format for a situation that benefits from the presence of a job aid.

Basic Rule 4

Job aids aren't the automatic solution for all information or memory problems. Although job aids are designed to deal with performance gaps due to information and memory issues, not all work settings are appropriate for job aid use.

Job aids aren't appropriate for all work situations involving information or memory either. Even if the performance gap is due to information or memory issues, there are times when a job aid doesn't fit. Typically, this will be because of the dynamics of the workplace or the nature of the performer.

Here are some of the work situations where a job aid is likely to be appropriate:

▶ *The sequence is critical to the success or failure of the task.* For instance, when installing a toner cartridge in a laser printer, you need to remove the cartridge tab before placing the cartridge in the printer. If you put the cartridge in the printer without removing the tab, it won't print or you'll have a laborious time removing the broken tab out of the printer path. If you find a job that involves work that must be done in a particular sequence (in some cases, this may be for insurance or legal requirements), then a job aid is usually appropriate. Sometimes managers insist that a particular sequence is critical, but this position might reflect their personal belief that "My way is the right way." In fact, there might be multiple approaches or sequences that lead to an acceptable result. As a general rule, the more "white collar" the nature of the task is, the more likely it is that there is a great variety of appropriate ways to successfully complete the work. Do not assume that just because the client or subject matter expert (SME) insists on a particular sequence that such a sequence is indeed the only or even best manner to do the work. Test this assumption.

▶ *The job aid enhances the confidence of the performer.* There are times when the presence of a job aid encourages the worker to be more confident and perform better. This might happen even when the performer doesn't need to use the job aid; just the knowledge it is there boosts the worker's confidence. One example is a presenter who has notes on index cards: The speaker may never need to refer to the cards but their presence will likely reduce the speaker's fears and improve the quality of the presentation. In other cases, a performer might not be willing to admit that a job aid would be valuable—especially around issues like confidence. You might encounter a situation where the performer doesn't express a need for a job aid and doesn't appear to be especially deficient, but the presence of a job aid would improve the speed and consistency of work because it serves as a safety net.

▶ *The consequence of worker error is high.* There are some tasks where a mistake is extremely costly or once a mistake is made it can't be undone. Some examples include air traffic control or bomb disposal and disarmament. Under such circumstances, a job aid makes sense. You want to do whatever is possible to reduce the chance of a mistake because the effect of the error would be so great. There is a range of different formulas and approaches to determine the consequence of an error. Some of these approaches also factor in how likely or frequent a mistake could be. Whatever approach you use to determine if the consequence of error is high, be sure to evaluate across the work process or extended enterprise. A relatively "minor" error on an assembly line could have major consequences because it forces others on the line to hold up production to compensate for it, thereby affecting the performance of everyone else.

▶ *The task is rarely used or infrequently performed.* If a particular job is something that a performer doesn't do very often, then memory is likely to become an issue. Workers might have to remember passwords that they don't use frequently or work sequences that are needed only once a year. In such instances, the likelihood of forgetting is great. So, as a general rule, when a task isn't used very often, it's a good candidate for a job aid. This is one of the most important and best justifications for developing a job aid. Workers may insist that they "know" the information, but if they don't have to use it frequently, you should start by assuming that accurate recall is likely to become an issue and then confirm that assumption.

▶ *The task is easy to get wrong.* When it's easy to make a mistake doing a particular job, then you'll want to identify ways to minimize the errors. A classic example of this might involve a new performer called to distinguish between particular pieces of action or decisions. For instance, a customer care representative in a call center might have to decide on the spot whether to authorize a full refund to a customer, allow a return of a problem item, or disallow any returns and refunds. In this instance, a Decision Tree would provide excellent support to help ensure that the new worker makes the correct choice. Thus, job aids are one attractive option when a task is difficult to do correctly. Assuming that the problem isn't with the performer (who might not be motivated to do the job well) or that a redesign of the job isn't an option (it may be easy to make an error because the work is poorly designed), a job aid is a good way to reduce mistakes.

▶ *The job depends on frequently changing information.* Sometimes it's too difficult to always keep people in the loop on a face-to-face basis because information changes so frequently. For instance, details about who is in the office on a particular day or which staffers are available to take calls are likely to change constantly. To hold staff meetings or to broadcast over a loudspeaker with updates isn't realistic for most work environments. However, a board at the front of the office that shows who is "in" or "out" or a panel on the office phone that indicates whose lines are busy (and can't take calls) are both examples of job aids that adjust to provide information that changes constantly. Given the rapid rate at which information changes, the importance of job aids as a means of providing updated information is critical. If a combination of turnover and revolving partnerships with firms outside the company results in constantly changing phone numbers and contact information, then employees can't be expected to try to stay current with these changes. Instead, a job aid that captures these changes (so workers can focus on remembering data that is less likely to change) becomes invaluable. Additionally, the range of possible EPSS options to provide this information continues to expand as ingenious variations on technology are adapted. Using pagers, PDAs, and wireless phones or capturing such information through scheduled hot-sync operations or network updates are all increasingly popular.

▶ *A job aid is a superior alternative to some training.* In theory, training addresses knowledge and skills issues, whereas job aids focus on information and memory performance problems. In reality, training is thrown at a wide range of performance problems, many of which aren't about knowledge or skills. Sometimes what is labeled training is really about providing information to performers who already have the skills to do the work. For instance, many shorter workshops that involve no skill building may be replaced or shortened by job aids. A seminar on new accounting procedures for finance officers is probably better served by spending less time in training and more emphasis on job aids. In such cases, a job aid might be a faster, less expensive, and more effective way of providing that information.

▶ *A task is complex but can be easily described in detail.* If a job lends itself to explanation or if it's possible to break it down, then a job aid is a good fallback resource to have. For instance, a Match job aid (by providing a finished or correct copy to compare work against) can be an effective way of simply clarifying what the product is supposed to look like. In some cases, however, the task is simple and explaining it through a job aid would slow the performer. Other times, a task is so complex, usually because of multiple paths or options, that it doesn't lend itself well to description. In those cases, avoid using a job aid.

▶ *A task requires a large body of information to be completed successfully.* Some work requires a tremendous amount of information for the performer to complete the task. In such cases, a job aid is a good fit. This is especially true when the performer is new to the job and is still assimilating the information. Keep in mind that the job aid in this situation doesn't need to provide all of the information. Instead, you might consider using a job aid to remind the worker about the most critical data that the task relies on or the information that is rarely used and, therefore, most likely to be forgotten. Job aids can also be used to help spur recall (by using an acronym). The key point is that information-intensive tasks usually benefit from the presence of job aids.

Think About This

Whenever training is initially prescribed, check to see if a job aid might be a superior solution. In many cases, the use of a job aid will at least shorten the amount of time (and expense) involved with the training. In some cases, the "training" isn't about providing more skills or new knowledge but is really focusing on new information, which can be provided more efficiently, cheaper, and faster with a job aid.

Basic Rule 5

You must always have a good understanding of the work setting the job aid is to be used in. Without knowing the job environment, you can't evaluate whether a job aid will be appropriate.

When Not to Use a Job Aid

There are also some circumstances when a job aid isn't going to be successful because of the work setting:

> *The job aid could damage credibility.* A worker with a job aid posted prominently at his or her workstation might be perceived as less competent by his or her peers. A performer who stops to refer to a job aid during work in a group may draw ridicule from co-workers who don't feel the need to turn to their notes. Sometimes peer pressure prevents performers from using job aids that they need and could benefit from. A training course is often a poor means to determine if the job aid will damage credibility. Participants might be willing to try new skills or experiment in the class, but then, for a variety

of reasons, fail to use those same skills at work. A job aid that appeared comfortable to use in a training class might be scorned in the work environment.

▶ *The job aid would slow down performance.* There are many work settings where use of most job aids is not realistic because it would distract from the job or force the worker to perform slower. For example, imagine trying to drive a car at high speeds on a congested road while referring to directions on a piece of paper. This behavior would be unsafe for the vast majority of drivers. Job aids, under certain circumstances, might slow performance by forcing the worker to reduce the pace of work, interrupt the work to refer to the reference, or go slower for safety reasons. In many work scenarios, such as an assembly line or a job where pace is critical, it isn't possible to allow repeated interruptions in service to check a job aid. In these cases, the job aid either needs to be usable without interrupting the task or a job aid isn't likely to be a viable option. If it isn't possible to use a job aid, the solution is likely to involve either getting the performer to memorize the relevant information or reworking the job so this is no longer an issue. Reworking could mean changing the nature of the work, dividing the task into subtasks, or automating the work.

▶ *The environment doesn't lend itself to a job aid.* This is a catchall category that recognizes sometimes the performer is likely to be in a situation where it isn't possible to bring a reference or job aid along. For instance, when a worker performs in a very fluid work setting (such as visiting a range of client sites), it might not be possible to predict what job aids would be appropriate. Or, the performer might be a power worker, for example, who must repair utility lines at night in a thunderstorm, making it difficult or impossible to rely on a job aid. The rain, thunder, darkness, downed electrical wires, and the need for mobility in the field would make most conventional job aids unrealistic for this environment. Other workers have to carry everything needed for the job while making field visits (such as a social worker or police officer walking a beat or mail carrier on foot). They simply can't afford the weight of one more item that must be carried or stored someplace. These are all examples where the environment doesn't lend itself to many job aids. It's critical to be realistic about the work environment and the challenges it presents to job aid usage. Given that caveat, don't assume that just because the environment is challenging, high tempo, or fluid that a job aid is absolutely not workable. Very intense and high-stress work environments may increase the need for job aids (because the tempo and pressure result in reduced recall as human memory and processing ability is lowered). Such situations call for creativity on your part as a designer to create a job aid that is functional despite an environment that makes usage difficult.

▶ *Consulting a job aid might decrease customer confidence.* Imagine going in to see a medical professional for treatment and having the doctor or dentist continually refer to a job aid on how to conduct the particular procedure you need. For many patients, who might be suffering already from anxiety, such a sight would reduce the confidence they held in their medical provider. In such work settings, even if the worker would perform better with a job aid, the visibility of the job would likely reduce customer confidence. Therefore, in some settings, the most valuable job aids are the ones that are imperceptible to the public.

Noted

One restaurant found that with a constantly changing menu, servers were unable to remember the daily specials. Yet customer surveys indicated that when servers had to read specials from a pad of paper, the specials were perceived as less appetizing because the server didn't seem to be as enthusiastic about them. The solution? The restaurant posted daily specials on chalkboards above the tables at several strategic locations around the restaurant. In this fashion, the servers could refer the customers to the chalkboard, and the server and the customers could read through it simultaneously with the server making comments on each special. This preserved the server's credibility and orders of specials increased. This is one example of how a lack of customer confidence was a factor with the initial job aid (specials on a pad of paper carried by the server).

▶ *Performer memory is a superior option.* It might be easier to write something down or produce it as a job aid, but because of various work restraints (such as customer confidence, peer pressure, or difficulty in accessing the job aid when needed), there are times when the best option is to expect the performer to memorize the information. You can probably guess examples where memorization is a bad idea: when information changes frequently, when the information is complex, or when the information is used infrequently and, therefore, forgotten easily. You will get more details in chapter 4 about how to determine whether you should expect the employee to memorize the information or go with a job aid instead.

Selecting the Appropriate Format

You've followed the advice in the preceding sections and you've determined if the performance gap and work setting are appropriate for a job aid. But, which format to use? Table 3-1 provides some advice you can use to choose among the 10 job aid formats you read about in chapter 2.

Table 3-1. Choosing among the 10 job aid formats.

Job Aid Format	When It's Appropriate
Reminder	Use this format when the work environment is complex and you want to keep job support as simple as possible so you don't add to the complexity of the task. This can also be a good, quick, improvised job aid. (Think back to the Apollo 13 example from chapter 2.) It is good in situations where you need something right away but don't have time to call in help to produce it. This is also an appropriate format when you're worried about slowing up performance because typically the Reminder job aid consists of only a few words or a symbol (such as an arrow reminding a mail sorter to keep the package pointed up). Finally, use this format if you are considering integrating the job aid into a tool or piece of equipment (such as a tire that lists the inflation tire pressure or a copy machine that has a page text symbol embedded into the plastic to remind users to feed documents face down).
Match	A Match job aid often takes the form of a picture or a scale model or replica. The purpose is to give a performer a clear comparison of items produced to the desired result. A Match job aid is appropriate for a number of situations. When workers have a range of linguistic expertise, then pictures or models will often be clearer than texts. Match job aids are also highly appropriate when there is only one type of acceptable result or product. To do this, the performer usually needs to compare an item to see if it meets a set standard or is of acceptable quality. Therefore, Match job aids are useful for quality control. Match job aids are also good to use with new performers who haven't developed the expertise to judge if the final product meets specifications.
Step	Whenever the task involves a series of steps, a Step job aid is appropriate. Rather than focusing on the outcome (what the finished product looks like), the Step job aid is good for workers who are still learning the process. A Step job aid is also good when the sequence of steps in a task is critical.

(continued on page 48)

Table 3-1. Choosing among the 10 job aid formats (continued).

Job Aid Format	When It's Appropriate
Checklist	If there is a series of actions a performer needs to do before the work is complete (or before moving on to another aspect of the task), a checklist is an effective format. This is especially true if many of the actions are mundane and done repeatedly by the worker, making it easy to forget what steps were done this time or the last. Use a Checklist job aid to be sure that nothing is forgotten. Additionally, Checklist job aids are also sometimes used for quality control. If a manager isn't able to observe a worker actually doing the task, utilizing a checklist is also a form of oversight, much like punching in with a time card. Finally, Checklist job aids can be useful for jobs that are very stressful for the performer, especially a new performer doing the task for the first time. By going through the checklist shortly before performing, the worker is reassured that everything is in order. For instance, military paratroopers will typically stand and go through a parachute/ equipment check shortly before exiting the airplane; this checklist is theoretically aimed at spotting problems with parachutes and equipment but is actually focused more at reducing anxiety and reassuring the troops before they parachute into combat.
Worksheet	There are three primary instances in which Worksheet job aids make sense. First, if calculations or mathematics are involved, a Worksheet job aid is very appropriate. It can reduce the likelihood of error. Second, if you want to get performers to use standard formats for their work, a Worksheet job aid can encourage people to follow a particular process or use a specific format to complete a task. Third, if there are a variety of ways to reach a particular result (so a Step job aid isn't appropriate), a Worksheet job aid can provide an example showing new performers one correct method of doing the calculations. Worksheet job aids are primarily used with paper and electronic media.
Process Table or Flowchart	Use this job aid if there is a sequence to be followed but unlike the Step circumstances, you can't be sure where the performer will start. This is because the performer may need to consult a particular aspect of the process (such as where the work goes after the performer is finished with his or her role) rather than starting at step one. Additionally, use a Process Table job aid when you want to provide a big picture or overview of all of the work rather than just a limited task.
Decision Tree	This format is appropriate when a worker is faced with several different options and must distinguish between the various options to choose the right answer. For instance, when a manager is trying to determine which disciplinary action is appropriate for an employee's misbehavior, this type of job aid would help the manager determine what kind of violation the misbehavior was and what actions should be taken in response. A Decision Tree job aid is also effective with new workers who have not developed the experience to differentiate among alternatives; it guides performance by reminding the new worker of the critical factors that distinguish the various elements.
Troubleshooting Diagram	Use this format when a performer must diagnose a problem and work through several stages or levels of diagnosis by eliminating symptoms and digging deeper to reach the correct answer at each level of diagnosis. Typically, what differentiates the circumstances in which a Decision Tree would be used versus a Troubleshooting Diagram is that a Decision Tree would determine the correct answer from among a range of alternatives. But, a Troubleshooting Diagram would involve eliminating a range of alternatives, then focusing on the remaining option to eliminate another level of options and so on.

Job Aid Format	When It's Appropriate
Troubleshooting Diagram (continued)	until the root cause or problem is identified. The Troubleshooting Diagram usually involves complex situations with multiple stages of analysis, or it uses a process of elimination to generate the correct answer. The Troubleshooting Diagram is a good means of encouraging a systematic approach to a problem, which is good for inexperienced or undisciplined performers.
Data Array	A Data Array job aid is best used when there is a pool of information from which an employee needs to pick from. The Data Array does not try to get the performer to use a particular process or to work through the problem. The Data Array could simply be a list of phone numbers or employee names and job titles. Use a Data Array job aid when information is not worth remembering; if it's easier to put it on a job aid than remember; or if the information tends to change frequently because of office turnover, organizational changes, and so forth.
Script	This job aid is appropriate in a number of circumstances. First, if an employee is new and tends to be halting or unpersuasive in delivering a particular message, a Script job aid can provide the words that the employee needs to say. Second, if precision in what the worker says is critical, a Script job aid makes a great deal of sense. By providing a copy or a shorthand version of what needs to be said, this job aid increases the likelihood that what the performer says will be exactly what is supposed to be said.

Of course, there will also be times when you will want to combine formats (so it is a hybrid Script–Decision Tree job aid). Deciding which format to use is a function of assessing the work environment (and the barriers to particular job aids) and an analysis of the task involved with the performance gap. Job aid 3-1 is a tool you can use as a quick reference guide to the different formats of job aids available to you.

Bundled Versus Stand-alone Job Aids

One of the decisions you'll also face is whether to provide just the job aid or to combine the job aid with other interventions (such as training, organizational restructuring, or different company benefits). It's important to let the front-end analysis be the driver for this decision. Front-end analysis involves determining what matters to the business, establishing the nature of the performance gap, assessing possible causes of the performance gap, and proposing solutions that are likely to have an impact on closing that gap. Instructional designers or trainers may turn to job aids because they take less time than training or because the designers are more comfortable with developing job aids than they are with changing a process or rewriting policies or redefining the work. Choose a job aid because it's appropriate for the performance gap, not because it falls within your comfort zone.

JOB AID 3-1: Job aid format selection.

Use this job aid to choose the appropriate format for the work setting you're dealing with.

If...	And...	Then Use This Format
...you need a model or example to compare to	⟶	Match
...the sequence is critical	...the performer will start at the beginning	Step
...you want to confirm that nothing was left out...	...the sequence isn't critical	Checklist
...wording or phrasing is critical or must be exact	⟶	Script
...the task involves calculations or filling in the correct answer	⟶	Worksheet
...you want to encourage a particular approach or format (but can't require it)	⟶	Worksheet
...there are multiple pieces of data that the worker selects from...	...the data changes frequently	Data Array
...there are multiple pieces of data that the worker selects from...	...it's easier to create a job aid than to memorize the information	Data Array
...must diagnose or choose the right answer from among several options	⟶	Decision Table
...must diagnose or choose the right answer from among several options...	...and then proceed to one or more levels of other options to select the right answer	Troubleshooting Diagram
...the correct sequence is critical...	...the worker might not be starting at the beginning step	Process Map
...the correct sequence is critical...	...the worker needs a "big picture" perspective on the process beyond the task	Process Map
...the worker only needs to remember a single piece of data...	...there is no sequence, process, order, or format requirement	Reminder

By conducting a front-end analysis, instead of just throwing a range of activities (some training, a couple of job aids, a team-building activity, and perhaps a motivational speaker) at a problem and hoping that at least one of the interventions works, you'll be choosing solutions that have a real chance of solving the problem.

The second factor that drives the decision about whether to bundle job aids with other interventions is your evaluation component. Specifically, there are two elements to the evaluation equation. First, you may discover that although a job aid alone will not solve the performance problem, it will reduce it and a job aid alone may have a much higher ROI than a bundled set of activities (such as training, a job aid, and some team building or coaching). Second, for evaluation purposes you may choose to implement the activities separately (rather than concurrently) so you can evaluate the impact of each. This level of evaluation is important if each of your various options is expensive to roll out and you're trying to determine the relative impact of each intervention (both to justify that action and also see if it makes sense to delete one of the solutions from the overall package). By implementing each intervention separately, you might improve your ability to isolate the impact of each solution.

Finally, you should never forget that many job aids require training of their own. It usually isn't sufficient for you to just hand a group of employees a job aid and tell them to use it. Try this approach and you are likely to have just produced an expensive and unique coaster for drinks. In many cases, you'll need to train performers on the job aid itself if you expect them to use it and use it appropriately. In many cases, such training on how to use the job aid will determine whether performers feel comfortable turning to it during work or whether use of the job aid ends up interrupting the task and thus slowing performance. What you'll likely discover is that the cost of producing a job aid and then training workers for two hours on its use has a far better ROI than taking the same pool of employees and sending them to a three-day training class sans job aid or just passing out a job aid.

Issues to Consider With Technology

One of the wonderful opportunities to exploit with job aid design is the wide range of options that have emerged as technology has become ubiquitous. From PDAs and wireless phones to GPS systems within delivery trucks (to provide maps for drivers and track compliance with delivery schedule) to automated tasks to EPSS, the range of and reliance on technology for work only continues to grow. The presence of technology and growing reliance upon it provides both opportunities and challenges for you as a designer of job aids.

It is especially critical when using technology—whether to deliver the job aid or to serve as an information repository—to focus on how user friendly the technology is and to be able to integrate all this into the work setting. Here's some guidance for you to consider when you base job aids on technology:

▶ *Use a particular technology because it fits the work environment.* As obvious as this advice sounds, there is a tendency among many organizations to force-fit job aids into technology because the company has the technology available, with little regard for the appropriateness for work setting and the ability to match job aid to technology. This may happen because management falls in love with a particular delivery medium. For example, a touch-screen database that helps users troubleshoot problems can be a wonderful resource if the work environment lends itself to using the computer and the task allows for interruptions. If the task doesn't allow for interruption or access to and use of a computer screen is problematic, it's a wonderful toy that users will avoid.

▶ *Consider technology dispersion issues.* Job aids designed to operate in particular software platforms may exclude part of the workforce if some performers have older computers or earlier versions of the software. A job aid that is disseminated through a PDA or wireless phone may face incremental implementation if the organization replaces devices gradually rather than all at once.

▶ *Determine variance in user expertise.* Testing performer and work setting issues is more complicated when technology is involved. You can expect a wide range in the level of knowledge and expertise in most workforces when it comes to familiarity with a range of technology. Effective use of job aids delivered or embedded within technology will usually account for these differences.

▶ *Support issues become more complex.* Importing a job aid into the network or adding it to a Website or creating a pull-down screen with a software program adds to support issues. As a job aid designer, you're responsible for creating the job aid, but who "owns" the responsibility for converting or adapting the pull-down menu when the organization changes the software the menu resides in? Who will update the job aid content on the Website after your contract has expired? These problems can usually be resolved, but they require partnering with IT, operations, human resources, or other functions within the organization.

▶ *Contingency planning is important.* Some technology is so reliable and ubiquitous that this issue becomes moot; the organization naturally develops backups to the system anyway, so the job aid is robust. For instance, many white-collar professionals have come to rely on wireless phones as a key work tool. However, some secure facilities don't allow visitors to bring in wireless devices or laptops for meetings. If you depend upon wireless phones to send text messages to staff members about critical schedule changes, you have to recognize that sometimes the phone will be outside the network, in a building without coverage, or out of power. This becomes a problem if that scheduling is critical for performers, but the technology delivery method isn't redundant.

Noted

Technology provides some wonderful opportunities to support workers and offer access to job aids. It is important to select a particular medium as a delivery mechanism because it fits the work environment and is appropriate for the job aid.

Getting It Done

Now that you've had an opportunity to get some sense of what a job aid is and the potential value a job aid can provide, exercise 3-1 can help you apply the content from this chapter.

Exercise 3-1. Identifying the best job aid format for the work setting.

1. Identify at least two performance gaps at your job or with a client where a job aid would not be an appropriate solution. What is it about the work context that makes it unsuitable for a job aid?

(continued on page 54)

Exercise 3-1. Identifying the best job aid format for the work setting (continued).

2. This chapter pointed out nine different circumstances where a job aid would be appropriate. Identify at least two work situations where a job aid could be an appropriate solution.

3. One of the work situations where a job aid is not likely to be a good fit is one where the performer is not willing to use it (perhaps because of peer pressure or fear of appearing uninformed). Think of your own work. Is there a particular task or work setting where your pride or peer pressure would discourage you from using a job aid? Is so, how could you design a job aid to minimize that resistance and make it more acceptable to utilize a job aid?

4. Think of at least one instance you've seen where technology was used to provide information yet the medium was inappropriate for the purpose because it was distracting or interrupting the task or because it wasn't capable of accurately conveying the information. Think of at least one instance where technology could be an effective means for embedding or delivering a job aid for a particular task.

Starting with chapter 4, you're going to begin practicing the book material by designing your own job aids.

4

The Job Aid Development Process

What's Inside This Chapter

Here you'll:

▶ Find out about the sequence for developing a job aid
▶ Examine practical considerations involved with each step of the process
▶ Practice applying the process by developing a job aid of your own.

Developing a Job Aid—The Process

What's the process for creating a job aid? How do you begin? It's a little more involved than just deciding that a job aid is a good idea or turning to it as a last resort when you realize you've got to cut the length of training. Just as performance consulting involves a systematic, results-based approach and as instructional systems design involves a systematic process to assess training needs and develop solutions, the process for developing a job aid is also systematic. It doesn't have to take a long time, but it's critical to follow the process. Otherwise, you will end up generating reams of paper-based job aids and expensive electronic task supports that clutter workspace and bog down workers rather than boost performance. The job aid development process ensures that you'll develop job aids that make sense, fit the worker and the work situation, and boost productivity.

The Job Aid Trigger

The job aid development process starts with a trigger—something that provides the indication or justification that initiates the process of developing a job aid. That "something" can come in one of several forms:

> ▶ *A front-end analysis identifies a task that requires a job aid due to memory or information issues.* A front-end analysis is a systematic review of critical organizational objectives, the performance necessary to achieve those goals, any performance gaps that exist, and what is causing those gaps. A front-end analysis is typical of the work that a performance consultant would do when engaged by a client to determine why a performance problem exists and what to do about it.

> ▶ *A task analysis identifies several training elements that should be converted to job aids, often as a means of shortening a course.* A task analysis is often done by an instructional designer prior to developing training. A task analysis (table 4-1) involves determining the key steps for a particular role or piece of work and the skills necessary to perform it (Piskurich, 2000).

> ▶ *A manager decides that creating a job aid is a better way to provide information than relying on a meeting or training.* Remember that job aids address informational problems. There are many ways for organizations to provide information. For example, a manager might call meetings or issue memos reminding employees about particular data. Or, a manager could walk around the worksite, seeking to pass on critical information to employees about new priorities, new orders, customer feedback, or changes in work procedure. In such cases, a manager might decide that a job aid is a superior means of passing on that information so the manager doesn't become the information conduit and so that the employee isn't required to remember the details.

> ▶ *An instructional designer has been asked to develop a job aid as support for training.* On occasion, an instructional designer or trainer develops training

Table 4-1. Task analysis.

What is a task analysis?	A task analysis breaks down a complex task into its components—the steps involved and the knowledge required. To do a task analysis, you observe the work and interview an SME or key performer.
What do you want to identify in a task analysis?	• Why someone would learn the skill • Prerequisite skills, knowledge, and attitudes • Special materials or tools required • Warnings of dangers, both overall and at specific points in the process • The critical steps (no more than five to seven, otherwise you should split it into another task) and the sequence of the steps • Whether the sequence is critical or flexible • Any other steps necessary to complete the task and their sequence • How critical any given substep is • Conditions that must be satisfied before going on to the next step • Reasons for doing steps at a particular point • Signs of success for each step (for confirmations) • Signs of failure for each step
What is the process for doing a task analysis?	• First review any documentation, manuals, or process maps you have on the task • Second, observe at least one expert and take notes as you observe • Either slow down experts during the task to ask questions or interview afterward • Identify each step • Document what you saw and what the expert told you, then ask for the SME's reaction—there will almost always be gaps identified • Expect the process to be iterative
What should you ask the SME?	• What is the SME doing? • Why is it important/what is the rationale? • Why is the SME doing it that way? • Is there a warning necessary? • How does the SME know what to do next (if there is a choice between two or more actions)? • How can the SME tell if a step was done right? • How can the SME tell if a step was done wrong or incompletely? • Is the sequence critical? • What does the SME do that isn't documented?

material and realizes that some of the content will require reminders after the participants leave the workshop. Other times, pressure to shorten the workshop means that the trainer can expose the participants to particular skills or processes but doesn't have enough time to internalize them with the participants, hence, the need for a job aid to compensate for the lack of memory. In these cases, the job aid is designed to support the training. Although the training provides the knowledge or skills, the job aid helps the performer remember what the class covered and how to use it.

Basic Rule 6

The decision to develop a job aid can be justified on the basis of one of these four prompts: a front-end analysis identifying a memory or information problem, conversion of some training content that is informational in nature, a manager's decision to convey information through the job aid rather than a meeting, and as support for training content.

The foregoing examples are legitimate triggers—reasonable and justifiable reasons for turning to job aids. However, it's not a reasonable trigger if it's simply a request by a manager. Also, a decision to not train at all in the hope that a job aid will provide the skills instead should not be a trigger. If the employee truly lacks the knowledge or skills to perform a particular task, a job aid usually won't be sufficient. Job aids work when someone already knows how to do the work. So job aids are not a cheap substitute for training. Sometimes decision makers use job aids as an economy measure to address a performance problem even though the job aid is inappropriate for that particular performance issue. Therefore, it is important to recognize that only some actions can be reasonable and legitimate triggers of a job aid development process. Just because someone asks for or demands a job aid doesn't mean it will be an effective fix.

The Job Aid Development Process

Once the need for a job aid has been demonstrated, the process for developing a job aid begins. The process is important because it is tempting to take shortcuts when developing job aids because of their apparent simplicity. But, taking shortcuts leads to creation of job aids that don't work, aren't used, or are inappropriate for the performance issue they're expected to address. Consequently, it is critical to be systematic in developing job aids and follow the process consistently. This job aid development process consists of nine steps, which are described in greater detail in the sections that follow:

1. Collect task and performer data.
2. Confirm that a job aid is appropriate for the work setting.
3. Determine if training support is necessary.

4. Select the appropriate job aid format.
5. Design and develop the job aid.
6. Validate the draft job aid.
7. Troubleshoot the draft job aid.
8. Roll out the job aid.
9. Maintain and upgrade the job aid.

Step 1. Collect Task and Performer Data

This step involves defining the task and determining what is known about the performer and work situation. This is basically a task analysis or an abbreviated version of a task analysis. A task analysis involves identifying the steps that make up a particular task, and it provides an understanding of that work (Is there a critical sequence? What steps appear to be critical and what ones are optional? What competencies are necessary to perform this task?). This is not only important for design of a job aid but also crucial for design of a tool, creation of an EPSS, or development of training. The task analysis ensures that there is alignment between the job aid and the task (or the training and the task) and that extraneous material isn't included. There are a variety of methods for conducting a task analysis. The two most common ones involve observing performers on the job as they perform the task or interviewing an SME or an exemplary performer about the task.

Step 2. Confirm That a Job Aid Is Appropriate for the Work Setting

After undertaking a task analysis, you will have identified the steps involved in the task and have a clear understanding of what the performer must do to perform the

Noted

The task data that you gather should not only identify what steps are involved in the task, but also should address speed (How fast does the worker need to perform?), frequency (How often does the performer do the task?), complexity (How complicated is the task?), consequences (What happens if the performer makes a mistake?), barriers (What aspects of the work environment complicate the task?), stability (How likely is it that the task will change in the near term?), and difficulty (How easy or difficult is it to do the work?).

work successfully. But, the second step in the process means determining whether you should rule out a job aid and rely on another option instead. This involves several issues: Are there elements of the work circumstances that make a job aid inappropriate? Is the performance gap due to an information gap? Does it make more sense to rely on performer memory than a job aid? It's critical to confirm early in the process whether a job aid is appropriate. Otherwise, you could spend a great deal of time and resources (especially with multimedia or EPSS-related job aids) only to discover that they have been wasted.

Step 3. Determine if Training Support Is Necessary

Job aids are attractive to many managers and HR directors because they can reduce the amount of time spent in training. But a frequent mistake made by many decision makers is the failure to recognize that many job aids will require training on how to use the job aid. Step three of this process involves testing to see if the job aids will require training support to be effective. In short, do workers need to be trained how to use the job aid? This is an especially relevant question given many types of EPSS or software-based job aids. Job aid 4-1 can help you decide if training support is necessary to support a job aid.

Noted

Training support for a job aid refers to the degree of training workers may need to learn how to use the job aid. Generally speaking, job aids will fall into three areas when it comes to training support. Some job aids require no training support and can stand alone. Other job aids require introductory training that is usually short and is more likely to provide a context for the workers so they understand why the job aid is being deployed. The third area involves job aids that require extensive training. As more job aids involve various forms of technology, this is a frequent circumstance. In such cases, there is probably knowledge or skills that the job aid requires (such as the ability to use the database that the data array is part of or knowing key concepts or background knowledge necessary to make sense of the job aid).

JOB AID 4-1. Job aid training requirements.

Use this job aid to determine if the job aid needs training support and, if so, what degree of support is required.

For the job aid to be effective, does it require...

- Repeated practice, role-plays, or simulation?
- Extensive and detailed training or explanation?
- Introductory training or orientation only?
- No training support and is self-explanatory?

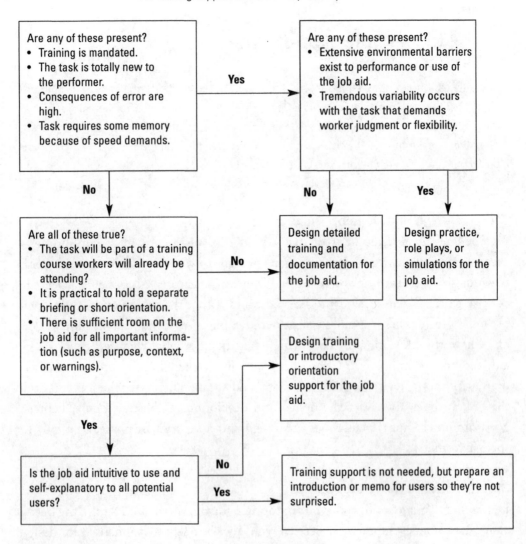

Step 4. Select the Appropriate Job Aid Format

The choice of job aid format is driven by the task analysis results. Once you've analyzed the steps involved in the work, the skills necessary, what support the performer needs, and the work situation (all of which are part of the task analysis), you're prepared to choose the correct job aid format. The task analysis process provides the background necessary to judge both the nature of the task and the challenges of the work environment. A fast-moving, chaotic work setting doesn't allow for a complex job aid.

Think About This

Many times job aid formats are chosen by default because the designer or SME is more comfortable with a particular approach. Design the job aid with the performer in mind. This means that steps to the task that a manager considers essential might actually turn out to be optional, even though the manager is insisting upon a particular order out of personal preference, not knowledge of what is truly essential.

Step 5. Design and Develop the Job Aid

The design and development of the job aid involves a host of responsibilities— everything from having project management skills to working effectively with SMEs to synthesizing everything you've learned from your task analysis to being a clear and concise writer. What is critical to keep in mind is that the design and development process for a job aid is usually a very iterative piece of work. Clients and workers often have trouble accurately conveying what they do, what they expect in the job aid, and how to improve it. Consequently, you will likely have to produce a partial draft, seek input, revise, seek input, revise, and so on. The better the job you do in the task analysis, the easier the design and development phase will go. Chapter 5 goes into much more detail about the design and development phase, especially for specific formats.

Step 6. Validate the Draft Job Aid

Determine that a job aid would be appropriate for the situation. Despite the best of analytical and development processes, you always need to validate your design. Basically, you're doing a pilot test of your job aid. A host of unanticipated issues can affect how successful the job aid will be once implemented across the workforce. Absent any effort to confirm the appropriateness of the design, these unanticipated issues can wreck even the best of designers. This initial test stage is your effort to account for the unexpected.

Basic Rule 7

No matter how good a designer you are, you can never anticipate all of the performer and environmental issues that are critical to the job aid design. Without an effort to validate the initial design, you might discover that many of the factors you failed to anticipate could prevent your design from being effective.

Think About This

Although the client might be in a hurry to pass out the job aid to everyone at work as soon as possible, there is tremendous value in running a limited pilot project first. Not only do you get a chance to identify ways to improve the effectiveness of the job aid, but also you make summative evaluation much easier. Summative evaluation addresses the organizational impact of an intervention. If you develop a job aid, you want to know if it helped the organization. By giving out the job aid to a pilot group (such as only one shift or one department), you make it possible to compare the two groups (those with the job aid and those without) and track any differences in performance—thus simplifying evaluation and controlling for some other variables.

Step 7. Troubleshoot the Draft Job Aid

The initial testing and piloting of the draft job aid always reveals unanticipated factors. The troubleshooting stage is where you control for those unanticipated problems by adapting and designing adjustments. You might discover that some of the troubleshooting issues don't involve the design per se but an organizational culture that discourages the use of job aids. In this case, the troubleshooting of the draft will highlight what changes need to occur if the job aid is to be effective.

Think About This

It is very easy in the troubleshooting phase to lose sight of the purpose of the job aid. You will likely get very diverse input on how to improve the draft job aid. Absent a clear, strong focus it is easy to be distracted and, in the effort to satisfy critics, produce a job aid that incorporates all of the design suggestions but ends up ignoring the original performance problem. The critical lesson for the troubleshooting phase is to stay focused.

Step 8. Roll Out the Job Aid

You've developed something you feel good about, you've tested it, and you've made modifications. Now, it's time to implement it. This is where many instructional designers and trainers drop the ball. Their focus is often on the design, assuming that (with a nod to the movie "Field of Dreams") "If you build it, they will come." It's just not true that if you produce something good, it will magically gain support. There are too many good job aids that were developed but never got acceptance from the workforce or management—proof that a clever job aid or creative design isn't sufficient.

The process of putting the job aid in the hands of the performers is a very situational one. The "right" approach varies from organization to organization. In some cases, you want to get the job aid to as many people as possible at the same time, thereby minimizing any perception of favoritism and reducing confusion that could result from supporting two different systems. In other instances you'll want a minimalist approach with incremental phase-in.

If your workforce is unionized, you'll want to involve the union representatives as early in the process as possible because they can play a large role in the degree of acceptance or resistance. Rollout also involves the question of how much support training (if any) is necessary for the job aid. But, the one absolute certainty that exists about a job aid rollout is this: If you simply pass out the job aid to workers with no buildup, no explanation, no support, and no effort to encourage usage, then it will be used by no one.

Step 9. Maintain and Upgrade the Job Aid

Many job aids enjoy initial success but eventually drift into disuse through a lack of support and failure to upgrade. Technically speaking, the care and maintenance of

Think About This

If it fits the organizational culture, a minimalist approach to implementation can be very successful. In this form of rollout, a few workers (or limited departments) receive the job aid. Others see it by accident as they interact with those who have the job aid. Through a combination of jealousy, curiosity, and turf wars, those without job aids demand a copy of their own. Even though you intended to provide the job aid to the entire organization anyway, you now find that everyone is clamoring for it. It is the difference between a corporate mandate ("Everyone will use the job aid and love it!") versus choice ("I want what they have!").

the job aid isn't part of the production process. But without this phase, job aids usually experience a short life. This is because most trainers, instructional designers, and performance consultants see themselves as responsible for creating the job aid and perhaps even implementing it. But, continued support is something that many of them would insist is someone else's duty; in the end, no one takes responsibility for maintaining the job aid. Consequently, it's not rare to find that workers can't get copies of a popular job aid past the initial rollout because no one wants to take responsibility for storage.

Maintaining and upgrading the job aid involves such issues as where to get replacement copies, who tracks the number of replacements a particular performer has been given, where to store extra copies of the job aid, and who is responsible for maintenance and repair of job aids that are not owned by individual performers (such as a template on a shared computer or a checklist on a motor pool vehicle. Even if you are not or cannot be responsible for the maintenance and upgrade of the job aid once it is released, you need to make provisions for these tasks in the design process.

An additional element to the maintenance and upgrade is evaluation of the job aid once it has been released. You'll engage in a formative evaluation during the design to improve the layout and usability, but you'll want to engage in a summative evaluation after the job aid has been released. This evaluation documents the impact of the job aid and also determines whether there is a need to upgrade or revise the job aid. If your summative evaluation shows a strong ROI for the initiative, you can also use this to garner supporter for an upgrade because of the demonstrated value to the organization of the job aid on performance.

Think About This

When you originally contract with the client to do this work, build in an agreement for an evaluation/follow-up piece to the work. In the absence of an agreement, there will be no upgrade phase. This needs to be more than just an agreement to "measure the success." Push the client for a commitment of resources so that you can evaluate and upgrade the job aid.

Putting the Process Into Practice

Now it's your turn to try walking through this process yourself. In the next couple of pages, you'll encounter a series of examples and cases that go through each step of the job aid design process so you can test your knowledge and practice your application. Following each question, you'll find a brief section entitled "Expert Guidance" to help you sort through the possible answers. In subsequent chapters, you'll have opportunities to practice applying what you've learned by designing your own job aids.

The Trigger

Scenario. Assume that you are a trainer or performance consultant employed by Alpha and Beta—a civil engineering firm. You've been asked by a senior partner in the firm to begin production of a job aid. This job aid is something that would be used by all engineers and technical staff in the organization. The purpose of the job aid is to remind employees of the correct procedure for starting and closing a new proprietary software program that the firm has developed for tracking billable hours by employee per client project.

But before you begin work on this job aid project, you need a legitimate trigger. It's not enough to develop a job aid just because a manager says so; this would lead to lots of wasted effort and job aids that actually would be performance inhibitors.

Which of the following would be a legitimate trigger for you to begin the job aid development process?

1. Management decided that rather than send employees to training on how to use the new software, Alpha and Beta would save money and time by just giving everyone a job aid about the software instead.

2. A manager's recommendation to develop the job aid based upon her observation that employees were incorrectly shutting down the program, resulting in data being lost or problems with startup for the next employee using the software.

3. A memo from the chief financial officer (CFO) about how important it is for employees to accurately track their billable hours so the firm can quickly and accurately bill clients. Therefore, the billable hours tracking software should be used appropriately.

4. Several team leaders request job aids for a group of employees who, because of work-related travel, missed the training courses on the new billable hours tracking software.

5. Indication that some of the material provided in the training course has been forgotten by employees so the job aid is designed to support the existing training.

Expert Guidance. Sometimes senior management requires you to do some work, and saying no just isn't an option. However, assuming that you have some ability to push back on client requests you believe are unreasonable, here is some feedback on each of the options you faced:

1. *Using a job aid to eliminate training:* This is probably not a legitimate trigger for a job aid development process. Just because a job aid might cost less money doesn't mean it is appropriate for the situation. The only instance where this is indeed an appropriate initiator for development of a job aid is if the training is entirely informational, meaning that it involves no new knowledge or skills. This may sometimes happen when software is updated and "training" is provided for employees to provide information on the changes in the program.

2. *Incorrect shutdown of program:* Again, this is probably not a legitimate trigger. The manager's observation may indeed be correct: Employees aren't closing the program correctly. However, you have no idea why employees are doing this. If they don't like using the program (a motivational issue), then providing more information (via a job aid) will change nothing. Job

aids deal with performance gaps due to information problems. If the observed shutdown problems are occurring because employees have forgotten how to close the program correctly, only then would a job aid be a possible option. But you would need to confirm this with a root-cause analysis.

3. *CFO memo on importance of tracking hours:* This is tempting because it indicates that the consequence of doing the task work might have significant consequences. But again, you don't know if the performance problem is due to informational problems or some other cause. Furthermore, despite the memo, you can't see if there is any financial consequence to the incorrect startup or shutdown of the program.

4. *Job aids for those who missed the training:* On its face this seems like a reasonable request. But, if the training involves skill and knowledge transfer, then job aids won't solve that. This is probably a stop-gap measure that might not correct the problem. If anything, it could make things worse because now management will be content that the problem (unskilled employees because of missed training) appears to be solved when, in fact, the problem could still persist.

5. *Training support:* This is the correct trigger. There may be skills or knowledge acquired in the training that requires reinforcement because employees can't remember everything they learned. In this case, a job aid is a good candidate, and this is also a reasonable request to begin the job aid development process.

Collection of Task and Performer Data

Scenario. Now is the time for you to analyze the nature of the problem that the job aid is supposed to address. Because you've received a reasonable justification for beginning the job aid development process, you need to begin by analyzing the steps involved in the task, the performer circumstances, and the environment potentially affecting the performance (as well as the use of the job aid).

Which of the following items would you want to include as part of the task and performer data phase for this job aid?

1. The frequency with which employees typically need to sign on and sign off of the program.
2. The steps involved in sign-on and sign-off procedures for the program.
3. The environmental factors that complicate the process of using the program (such as side conversations, distracting background noise, pressure to

complete the task quickly, glare from the morning sun on the terminal screen, and so on).

4. The degree of similarity of this program to any previous software that employees used to record billable hours.

5. The areas of the program that employees are the least familiar with.

Expert Guidance. Actually, this was a trick question. Remember, your trigger for this job aid process is that employees are receiving training on the software and you are responsible for developing a job aid to support the training. Any responsible training should have been based upon the task analysis that was used to develop the training. That task analysis would be necessary to determine what skills are required to use the software and what employees need to be taught in the class. You should be able to use the data from the analysis that was done to design the training. Your biggest challenge in this phase will be aligning the job aid with the training (so that the job aid serves as the memory jogger it's supposed to be rather than addressing tasks not covered in the training or handled sufficiently in the course so that no job aid is necessary).

If there was no task analysis done for the training (Shame on that instructional designer!), then the most critical piece of information you'd need for your job aid from the examples cited above would be option (2), "the steps involved in sign-on and sign-off procedures." For the purposes of this activity, you can assume that you've discovered that there are three steps involved in program sign-on and four steps involved with program sign-off. All these steps involve keystrokes on the computer keyboard in response to prompts on the computer screen.

Confirming That a Job Aid is Appropriate for the Job Setting

Scenario. In this instance, you know that a job aid is a given because it is being developed to support training employees will receive on the software. So, the usual question with this phase (Is a job aid the most appropriate way of improving performance?) isn't the question you need to answer. Instead, what you need to determine is what setting should the job aid be designed for? Because the job aid is to help with the training, you have a number of possible options:

▶ Locate the job aid near the workstation (which assumes that performers will be able to use it as they complete the task)

▶ Provide the job aid in training (which assumes it will be used to reinforce the training immediately by appealing to different learning styles and also provide an opportunity to discuss it during the training)

▶ Make the job aid available in work settings away from the task (such as a pocket card reference or screen reminder that provides a presence for workers). This approach assumes that you'll need to enhance memory away from the task setting because the nature of the task may make it impossible to refer to a job aid.

Think About This

Introducing the job aid in training can be an effective way to get performers comfortable with the job aid.

What are appropriate questions you would need to answer if you wanted to determine where the job aid should be used?

1. Does the presence of the job aid decrease client confidence in the worker by making the worker appear inexperienced?
2. Is the pace of the task too fast to allow performers to refer to a job aid during completion of the task?
3. Is the job aid likely to be self-explanatory and intuitive or will it likely require extensive explanation to show how it is relevant?
4. Is this a task that the worker typically does frequently?
5. How complex is the task?

Expert Guidance. Options (1) client confidence, (2) pace of the task, and (3) intuitive are all questions that could help you decide where to use the job aid. If the job aid reduces client confidence, then you need to find a way to hide it from customers or use it away from customers. Fortunately, that's not an issue in this instance—logging onto the software and inputting hours is done at the Alpha and Beta's office away from customers' eyes. The pace of the task determines if it's realistic to expect workers to step away from the work to refer to a job aid. In this case, the task isn't fast paced. How intuitive the job aid is determines whether or not it's essential to introduce it in training or with an orientation session.

The last two questions (frequency and complexity of task) are useful questions but not in this instance. If the task is rarely performed, it's a good candidate for a job aid because workers might have trouble remembering things that are done infrequently. If the task is complex, it might be difficult to remember accurately (especially for new performers) and is a good candidate for a job aid. But neither of these last two questions helps you decide whether the job aid is best used during the task, off site, or introduced in training.

Determining if the Job Aid Requires Training Support

This is a very important question to consider in most cases. Too often, managers assume that they can just hand out a job aid or have it magically appear on the computer or next to the tools, and people will figure out what to do with it on their own. You need to determine if the job aid requires extensive training or a simple orientation, is intuitive enough to be self-explanatory, or if it requires practice using (perhaps because of skills necessary for the job aid or if there are extensive environmental challenges that require practice with the job aid). However, in this hypothetical case, this question is already answered for you. The job aid exists to support training that is already occurring: You do not need to provide training to support the job aid, which is designed to support training. It should be designed so that it requires only a modest introduction or is intuitive to any potential users.

Selecting the Appropriate Job Aid Format

Scenario. You know that there are 10 different job aid formats. Given what you now know about the task, the work environment, and the performance gap, it's time for you to choose which format would be most appropriate for this job aid. You can assume that you've narrowed it down to the following five different formats. Which format would you choose?

1. Decision Table
2. Process Table or Flowchart
3. Checklist
4. Step
5. Reminder.

Expert Guidance. The Step format (4) would probably be the best option. Why? Based upon what you learned in the task analysis material above, the sign-in and sign-off processes involve several steps, and those steps need to be done in the correct sequence. A Decision Table (1) isn't likely to be useful because workers don't need to make any choices with this task. A Process Table or Flowchart (2) wouldn't be helpful because performers don't need a bigger picture of working with the program—only how to sign on and sign off correctly. Using a Checklist (3) could be effective by providing a list of what the worker must do to sign on correctly but still wouldn't be as effective as a Step format. The Checklist would not necessarily indicate a sequence. Last of all, the Reminder (5) is a reasonable format given that there are few steps to this task. However, because the steps to the task must be in the correct sequence and are divided into two different functions (signing on and signing off), it makes more sense to use the Step format.

Designing and Developing the Job Aid

Scenario. There many options for what this job aid might look like and what medium you might use to provide it. Assume that the steps involved in signing on and signing off the program are as follows:

▸ Start program: Hit keys [F3], then [Ctrl], followed by [Shift] + [F7], and the program startup screen will appear.

▸ Shutdown program: Hit keys [Alt], then [9], followed by [Y], and finally [F7], and the program screen will show "ending program—data saved."

Given this information, what would your version of the job aid look like?

Expert Guidance. There is a range of different media you can choose for a job aid like this. Imagine it as a plastic pocket card or a pull-down screen on a computer monitor. However, the simplest version would be a laminated piece of paper or plastic that is located at the workstation, perhaps on the side of the monitor or on the desk where the keyboard sits. The job aid could look something like job aid 4-2.

You'll notice how this job aid has a border around the content. The steps in it are numbered to point out the sequence. There is a clear label indicating the purpose of the job aid. The job aid provides a sense of what workers can expect if the sequence is followed correctly ("Program startup screen will appear."). The job aid text is concise with plenty of white space. These are all design elements about which you'll get more information on in chapter 5. There is, of course, more than one way to design this job aid so you should consider this example as just one of a number of possible versions.

JOB AID 4-2. Program startup and shutdown procedures.

Action	Do This:
1. Program Startup	1. Press [F3] key. 2. Press [Ctrl] key. 3. Press [Shift] + [F7] keys. Program startup screen will appear.
2. Program Shutdown and File Save	1. Press [Alt] key. 2. Press [9] key. 3. Type [Y] for "yes" to screen question of "Exit now?" 4. Press [F7] key. Screen will read "Ending program—data saved."

Job Aid Validation

Scenario. You will want to pilot-test the job aid to see whether it is user friendly. In this instance, your primary objective is to decrease the errors that occur when employees sign on and sign off the billable hours accounting software. You may select from a range of options to get feedback on the design. Here is the list that your director of human resources has decided is appropriate. You should choose one option from this list:

1. Give the job aid to a small but professionally diverse group of employees. Interview each one individually after he or she has had a chance to use the job aid several times.
2. Distribute the job aid and then send an email survey out to all employees asking for their input. Based upon the return rate, you can then extrapolate the degree of acceptance and approval for the job aid as well as see how much support there is for particular suggestions.
3. Sit near a workstation and observe staff as they access the software. Watch to see if they use the job aid during sign-in and sign-off procedures.
4. Get IT to establish monitors on all workstations that track whether it takes more or less time to sign in/sign off and how many restarts or

reboots occur during this sequence. Use this information to determine the ROI for the intervention.

5. Assemble a focus group of SMEs (IT staff and employees who already know the software well) and use their input to decide if the job aid is fine or not.

Expert Guidance. Choose option (1), small group of users with individual interviews. The purpose at this point is to find ways to improve the job aid. You don't care if it's popular or if there's agreement on what changes need to be made. You'll save the ROI analysis until after you've completed the modifications. For now, you just need to get feedback on how to make it more user friendly. Choice (2), distribute the job aid to all and email a survey, isn't bad, but by passing it out to the entire organization you run the risk that if you make revisions, outdated copies will continue to circulate.

Although from a political standpoint the survey is good because everyone gets a say, you also run the risk that some who are intimidated by the job aid or can't figure out how to use it will simply not respond so you won't hear from the people you with the most valuable data on improving the job aid. An interview allows you to read nonverbal behavior and probe if you think someone is holding out on you. You can also ask follow-up questions to get at user issues. Option (3), observation, is usually a good alternative, especially if it involves behavior that the worker may not be conscious of (such as ergonomic issues or ease of use or difficulty referring to the job while doing the task). Although observation often changes behavior that is relevant, in this case it would only be whether the performers choose to use (versus not use) the job aid. You'll still get useful insights about how easy it is for performers to use the job aid.

Troubleshooting the Draft Job Aid

Scenario. In this stage, you take the input you've received from the pilot version of the job aid and make corrections. What is the most critical issue you're likely to face at this stage?

1. Not enough time to make the changes you want to make.
2. Management sees no need to make any changes from the draft.
3. Input from the validation process is muddled and confusing.
4. The client has lost interest in the project.
5. The task has changed, so the original analysis is obsolete.

Expert Guidance. All these concerns are valid and realistic problems you might encounter as you incorporate feedback and revise a job aid. But, in this instance, the most likely issue is going to be (1), insufficient time. As you design job aids, you'll be under pressure to deploy them quickly. You will want to review feedback with your stakeholders or others involved in the planning process—and this takes time. Production logistical problems might affect your timeline, cutting into your ability to make all the revisions you think would be desirable. Clients, in particular, will pressure you for quick action and tend to err on the side of "Just do something!" Consequently, you might discover that some of your job aids are primarily a case of doing the best with the limitations that you face.

Rollout of the Job Aid

Scenario. You've garnered feedback on the draft version and made modifications as necessary. Now it comes time to implement the revised version. What are likely to be potential rollout issues to be concerned about?

1. Because you're not likely to "own" the workstations (they belong to other employees or departments), will the "owners" allow the job aid to be placed in a usable location on or near the computers?

2. Do you want to implement the job aid simultaneously or in a staggered fashion so that you'll have a control group to compare results with?

3. In the time that it has taken you to analyze the problem, design the solution, test it, revise it, and now roll it out, has management lost interest (and thus you've lost support)?

4. Will the training on the software be adjusted to alert participants about the job aid?

5. What has the organization's experience with job aids been like previously and how well did the workforce embrace them?

Expert Guidance. All of the above! Each of these questions is an important one to consider prior to rollout of the job aid. Rollout involves a combination of project implementation and change management. You must consider a host of issues involving logistics, communication, and resistance.

Maintaining and Upgrading the Job Aid

What issues do you suspect are likely to become factors over time with this job aid? What follows is a list of potential worries. Identify which one you think is most likely to be a concern.

1. The need to demonstrate ROI for this project after implementation is complete.
2. Keeping the job aids from becoming frayed, moved from the appropriate location, or used for other purposes (such as placemats, ice scrapers, an impromptu fly swatter, or a place to jot down phone numbers when a pad of paper isn't available).
3. Maintaining management support for the job aid.
4. Making revisions to the job aid and getting out the next version.
5. Determine where to store extra copies.

Expert Guidance. All these responses are good things to plan for during most job aid projects. In this situation, the correct answer is (2), degradation of the job aid. A job aid that is attached next to a worksite often tends to develop "legs" and walk away as workers use it for other purposes. As for concern (1), ROI, this is a project with minimal expenses and management support so it's not a good candidate for an ROI analysis. You may find it useful to do an ROI analysis just for political purposes ("Look how effective my projects are!"), but it's not likely to influence this particular job aid. As for (3), management support, once the job aid is implemented it is not likely to face much management resistance or need much support in the future. Option (4), future revisions, is a valid concern but not likely to be a factor in this case. Even if the software goes through changes, unless the log-on and log-off procedures change, there

Think About This

The best time to resolve who will be responsible for maintaining the job aid, storing copies, and replacing defective or broken versions is in initial discussions with the client. Raise this issue at the very beginning of the project.

will be no need to change the task. Storage (5) is a valid worry for many job aids. In this case, you'll probably need few spares, the job aid is likely to be small, and it could easily become the property of IT or the owner of the computers.

Getting It Done

Now that you've had a chance to look at the job aid development process from start to finish, try your hand at exercise 4-1, which has some activities to improve your practical skills.

Exercise 4-1. Reviewing the steps in job aid design and development.

1. Remember the four triggers discussed in this chapter as appropriate initiators for a job aid development process. Can you identify an instance where a job aid was developed but did not have one of those triggers? What was the result? Was the job aid effective, discarded, or irrelevant?

2. What do you believe is the most challenging aspect of the job aid development process? Why? What aspect do you feel is the least challenging aspect of the process and why? What skills do you feel you need to augment or improve for the most challenging aspect of the process?

3. Identify some additional strategies besides the ones mentioned in this chapter for validating a job aid to improve the initial draft.

4. What are some clever ways to validate an initial version of a job aid? How could you build in some quick methods for feedback on a job aid design?

This chapter has given you a look at the process of developing job aids. In chapter 5, you'll look in detail at the specifics of designing and developing a job aid. What are elements of a well-designed job aid?

5

Development and Design Tips

- -

What's Inside This Chapter

Here you'll learn tips for:

▶ Effective development of job aids
▶ Thoughtful design that accounts for the users' needs and the workplace environment
▶ Ways to work effectively with SMEs.

Building a Better Job Aid

Now you know a bit about the process of developing a job aid. Following that process ensures that you produce job aids that address performance gaps and have a realistic chance of improving the work that people do. But, you're probably still wondering about how to actually design a well-crafted job aid that makes the complex simple and the obtuse clear. That is the challenge—and the test—of a job aid. It should transform something that is difficult to grasp or complex to execute and reduce it in such a manner that a performer can master it and perform better.

Although good writing and effective design are arts, there are some basic ground rules that can help you create successful job aids.

General Job Aid Design Rules

The word "rules" is used loosely in the context of creating job aids. There are plenty of examples of effective job aids that don't follow these "rules." Additionally, under some circumstances, it isn't possible to follow this design advice. For instance, ideally a job aid provides a context by explaining when to start, what a good result looks like, how the performer would know if he or she is off track, why this task matters, and how it fits into the larger scheme or process of work. Often, however, it is not feasible to provide that much information—especially for a job aid that is supposed to be a quick reference so it doesn't interrupt the workflow. Consequently, you will oftentimes discover that you can't follow all of the "rules" because to follow one (provide graphic examples or illustrations) would conflict with another (provide plenty of white space and keep it simple).

Therefore, as you read through these design rules for designing job aids, keep in mind that almost no rules in this area are absolute. You'll need to make judgment calls about when to suspend a particular rule. Your task and environmental analysis is the best means you have of deciding which rules should take priority.

Appropriate Format for the Task

Different tasks require different formats. For instance, a Step job aid would be designed differently than a Match job aid. The media possibilities vary depending upon the format. For instance, a Match job aid could consist of a three-dimensional model or an exact replica of the finished product but that option isn't open for a Step job aid.

The first and most important rule for the design of a job aid is this: *The format must be suited to the job task.* Perhaps this sounds obvious and intuitive, but it's important to remind yourself of this rule. Failure to follow this rule can result in job aid formats that reflect the preference of the designer, not the needs of the performer.

Other Important Design Guidelines

Once you've got the appropriate format for the task, there are a number of other design considerations to take into account. The following sections address some of the most important ones.

Clear Name or Title

All job aids should have a clear, concise, obvious title located someplace on the job aid to attract the user's focus. Why is a name for the job aid important? The title provides a handle or reference for users so they can easily and clearly indicate what it is that is being referred to. Just imagine a worker saying, "Can I get a replacement for that laminated thing, you know, that thingamajig that is on the Velcro tab next to the computer, not the computer itself but near the CPU on the side, but not near the DVD tray, up higher than that, that thing that helps you with the password stuff. I'd show it to you, but it disappeared and I don't have a copy. Anyway, the old one's missing and I need a new one."

Ideally, the title should mention the task that it supports. Thus, a job aid that deals with conference participant materials might be called the "Participant Handout Checklist" or a Data Array job aid with lists of phone numbers and names that customers frequently need might be named "Customer Help Contacts" or "Frequently Requested Contacts." The key point is that the title allows someone who is in a hurry or multitasking on the job the ability to quickly determine if this job aid is relevant to the task. You can help the user by taking these elements into consideration as you design the job aid's title: placement (where on the job aid the title is), legibility (typeface and size of the title), and clarity (what the name of the job aid is and whether it makes sense to the user).

Explanation of Purpose

After the job aid title, you should provide a summary of the purpose of the job aid or some brief information about when to start or in what circumstances it will be useful. This provides context, especially if the performer is new, has had no training on the job aid, or has a wide range of job aids and tools to choose from. Some material that might be included in this piece of the job aid could be when to use the job aid, what materials are needed to start the task, how this task fits into a larger process, what circumstances the job aid is appropriate for, and the purpose of the job aid itself.

You are likely to view this element of the job aid as a compromise because you'll have to limit how much information you provide to keep the job aid manageable and concise. One guideline for making this decision will be where the job aid will be used. If the task is fast paced and the performer is supposed to refer to the job aid without interrupting work, then the explanation after the title needs to be limited or even nonexistent. If the job aid is something the performer can refer to before starting the task or during a brief work interruption, then a longer, more detailed explanation is appropriate.

Noted

When you show the job aid draft to SMEs as a means of validating the design, the SMEs will usually find the explanation about purpose to be redundant with the title. That's because the SMEs are very knowledgeable and likely need less information than most users. Remember that your job aid needs to work for all employees who do that task. The explanation of purpose should be more than just a regurgitation of the title; it should provide information that would be useful to new workers or those unfamiliar with the task.

Clear Language

It goes without saying that the job aid needs to be clearly written, but there are some specifics that will produce this clarity. For starters, use action verbs and an object for any steps. Avoid general words such as "analyze," "review," "consult," "coordinate," "communicate," or "process." Use action verbs that tell the performer explicitly what kind of action to take (table 5-1). The ideal verbs to use will come from the steps identified in your initial task analysis.

Providing the object in the statement is critical as well. It is not enough to tell participates to engage in a behavior or to do something; you should indicate what they are to do it to ("Read the Quick Start guide" or "Answer the question on the screen"). Use the active voice in your job aid writing, and write in short sentences or statements. Keep the language simple and concise.

Table 5-1. Sample action verbs.

Assemble	Enter	Measure	Reject	Save
Calculate	Examine	Observe	Release	Test
Calibrate	File	Push	Remove	Turn
Clear	Inspect	Read	Repair	Type
Count	Install	Record	Return	Write

Here's an example to show how important clear language is for job aids. Take a look at these three versions of the same step within a set of instructions:

1. The correct dosage should have been administered prior to eating.
2. Consume the prescribed amount before having food.
3. Swallow two pills before each meal.

The first version uses the passive voice. The second version uses an unspecific verb ("consume") that is potentially open to misinterpretation. The third version uses an action verb that is explicit to the required task. As you can see, even though each version refers to the same medicine and the same step, they imply significantly different messages. Only the third version makes it clear that the correct dosage is two pills, that they are to be swallowed (rather than chewed or dissolved), and that they should be taken before meals (instead of on an empty stomach or after snacks). Finally, the third version is more concise than the first two; being concise and precise is important for a job aid.

Think About This

If the nature of the task allows it, make sure the job aid also indicates what happens before and after each step. If the task is something the performer has never done before, this information helps align anticipation. The performer will have some idea of what to expect—and if he or she doesn't, that's a clear sign that something is wrong.

Intelligent Use of Graphics

When a wide range of fonts and typefaces became available on computers, some presentations and reports fell victim to the "hostage-note syndrome"—a graphic with a bewildering array of different looks and typefaces. Unfortunately, as graphics packages have proliferated and computing power allows for more photos and even video, the poor use of graphics in documents has grown into an epidemic!

Use graphics wisely in your job aids. First, for printed material it is generally better to use line art drawings than photos. The possible exception to this standard would be with Match job aids, in which a picture of the final product might be superior to a drawing. Even if the prototype renders clear images, you must remember that in the field there is a tendency to slap a job aid on the copy machine and crank out some copies, resulting in graphics (and production values) that grow fuzzier and less distinct with each copy cycle. Second, the distance from which the designer views the graphics is usually not the same distance from which the performer sees the graphics. As a result, graphic displays are often too small. Third, be absolutely sure that the graphics are relevant to the job aid and contribute to the understanding of the task. For instance, graphic images can often be an effective tool for job aids that must appeal to users with different languages. However, you must be sure that the image has a consistent meaning across performers' cultures. Although most trainers and managers recognize that many employees aren't native speakers, they frequently err by using images that don't have the same meaning in employees' diverse languages and cultures. Not only does this result in a confusing job aid, but also it reduces white space and makes the job aid harder to refer to during work.

Think About This

You must design job aids with likely support issues in mind. For instance, the initial version of the job aid may include a very clear, crisp picture of the final product. Unfortunately, as additional copies of that job aid are needed (because of new hires or because the job aid "walks away"), supervisors might simply go to the copy machine. Once there is a copy of a copy of the original job aid, that initial clear, crisp picture has been turned into a blur of dark pixels.

Emphasis of Key Concepts

It's important to use relatively few typefaces, fonts, and colors with any job aid so you can use contrast (such as a larger typeface or bold or a different color) to emphasize certain points. Also, depending upon how your job aid will be used, you'll want the distinct colors or typefaces to be able to quickly draw the worker's attention. If the job aid will be used while the performer is doing the task, you need to produce something that a worker can quickly glance to and find the right parts without searching or having to stop performing the task. If every line has a variety of typefaces or the entire job aid is a rich palette of color, the job aid might be eye-catching, but the worker is likely to have to search for the relevant spot. Information that is important should be highlighted or set in boldface type. Consider using a larger typeface for numbers in a Step job aid.

Basic Rule 8

Anytime a job aid is to be used without interrupting the work, the performer should be able to quickly glance over to the job aid and identify critical points. This requires concise writing and a visual style that makes it obvious where the job aid starts and what the critical points are.

Ample White Space

Job aids tend to place tremendous constraints on designers. Because the job aid might have to fit into a pocket or won't allow for scrolling so it must fit on one computer screen, you will often be forced into some rigid limits. Despite your desire to fit in more information, you can't make the card bigger or create a larger computer screen. Faced with such strict limits, designers look for other ways to sneak in more content. These can include reducing typeface size, changing margins, or cramming text together. These are all design no-no's.

Almost all job aids benefit from significant amounts of white space. Have wide margins. Put each step, bullet-list item, or decision point in a separate block or line. Use the space so that the eye is naturally drawn to critical points. The less white space there is on the page, the more clutter there is for the eye to sort through. Think of it this way: If the job aid were in a language you couldn't read, would you be able to quickly identify only through placement on the document what the critical points were?

It may be tempting to add extra content at the expense of white space, but the less white space you have on your job aid, the harder it is to use the job aid and the more mistakes workers will make with it.

Before-and-After Information

One of the critical content lessons is that the job aid should explain what the performer should expect before a particular step and what will happen afterward. Before you tell the performer to do something, it is helpful to explain if there are any conditions or circumstances that must exist before the step. This information can either serve to confirm to the worker that it's time to take the step, or it can help the performer identify the stage in the process the work is in. Often, the nature of the job aid won't allow much detailed explanation, but for tasks involving a great deal of judgment and for employees who are new to that work, this element (before-and-after information) is invaluable.

Small Steps

One common mistake designers make with job aids is combining steps because of space limitations. For instance, an instructional designer who has only a pocket card for presenting the information might try to reduce a 10-step process to four steps by combining separate actions. To an SME or an instructional designer who has spent a great deal of time studying a particular task, it might seem a reasonable space-saving device to write "Turn on the computer" at the risk of frustrating a beginner because the actual sequence would be:

1. Turn the power strip on.
2. Turn on the CPU by pushing the power button on the center face.
3. Turn on the monitor by pushing the green button on the front of the display.
4. Ensure the keyboard is plugged into the CPU.

For an experienced computer user, it's probably sufficient to say "Turn on the computer," but for anyone who has less experience or is unfamiliar with that particular workstation, a correct step-by-step breakdown is critical. Otherwise, the job aid will be a failure because it does not correctly show workers how to do the task.

It is critical that trainers and instructional designers don't take shortcuts with job aids. The failure to break down the task step by step is a common mistake that is usually made because of the pressure to fit material into limited space. You are better off developing an alternative to the job (such as expanding training or selecting a different medium to deliver the job aid content) than trying to combine steps for the sake of space.

Warnings Come First

Job aids are usually designed to be used while the worker is performing and often when the performer is in a hurry. It doesn't work to provide cautionary advice after a

Noted

As you read about the details involved in designing and developing job aids, remember this critical point: Your job is to make the task less difficult for the performer. The information from the task analysis and your understanding of the work environment can help you decide which elements to include on the job aid to make the task easier to perform.

step has been explained. The performer is likely to be focusing on the task and only occasionally glancing at the job aid. If there is something that the employee needs to beware of—especially if it could result in safety problems or task failure—that caution needs to precede the step. Typically, this warning is to alert the employee about the need for precision with a particular step because performing it incorrectly or out of sequence could have significant ill consequences.

The warning needs to be highlighted or emphasized in some fashion so that it stands out to the user. Some examples of the warnings that should precede a given step: safety threats, potential violations of rules or policies, reboot or start-over results (a mistake that forces the employee to start over), major consequences (an error could damage the system, sound an alarm, raise a security alert, or produce major problems), or common errors.

Think About This

If you need to provide a caution to the job aid user, you have several options. If the performer is going to use the job aid while performing, think about visual cues such as a different color or boldface font for the warning. If the job aid is to be studied prior to the task or if the performer can stop work to refer to it, think about using a warning that interrupts the use of the job aid or requires a positive action by the user. This could be a pull-down screen that requires a mouse click to proceed or an alarm that is turned off by pushing a key or button on a PDA.

Noted

A flooring company had a problem with customers continuing to use an abrasive cleaner on flooring tiles that were scored and damaged by the cleanser. The company put warning notes in the packaging when customers bought the tile advising them to avoid abrasives. This approach didn't work. The company then trained sales staff to remind customers as they purchased the tile not to use an abrasive when cleaning the tile. That didn't succeed either. The company then had letters printed on the tile that said "To remove this text, call 1-800-XXX-XXXX." Customers called the help line to find out how to remove the lettering and were told what cleaners to use but definitely to avoid abrasives. This solved the problem! The lesson from this story is that some successful job aids actually intend to interrupt the work or make it difficult to continue using the job aid until the worker confirms understanding or checks in.

Practice What You've Learned

You've had a chance to read through a number of points about designing an effective job aid. Now here is a chance for you to apply what you've just read to a job aid draft.

The Scenario. Analyze the example in figure 5-1 and identify how you could improve this job aid.

Expert Guidance. Granted, you do not know much about the task or performers for whom this job aid is intended. That lack of information makes it difficult to say exactly what is right and wrong in this job aid draft. Nevertheless, here are some points to consider:

1. The title of the job aid is weak. You can't tell what aspect of time management it would be useful for without reading the text of the job aid itself. There is no explanation of the purpose of the job aid or how it fits into a bigger picture or process. A new performer probably wouldn't be able to decide when to use the job aid or under what circumstances it would be appropriate or why it matters.

2. This is apparently a Checklist job aid. If so, the graphics to place the checkmarks in are too small and should be on the right side following the text. By placing the boxes (or circles) after the text, a job aid encourages the

Figure 5-1. Time management planning.

O Clear purpose established
O Work items have priority levels established
O Quadrant II items are identified
O "Stop doing" list created
O Sequencing of tasks determined
O Milestones for projects are clear and frequent
O All critical tasks are specifically delineated
O Complex steps are broken down into smaller steps
O Areas of responsibility are assigned and delegated when possible
O Start and end dates established

worker to read the item before checking something off. Putting the check boxes on the left-hand margin makes it easier to check them off without actually reading the material.

3. The clock adds nothing to the job aid. It does not clarify any of the checklist items and exists only to provide a graphic that reduces white space.

4. It appears that the job aid content is a poor compromise, although it's hard to know for sure without more task and performer details. The text is succinct but appears to combine some steps or questions. For instance, milestones could be "frequent" but not "clear."

5. If the checklist is intended to be used in reviewing a project to manage time (and thus the performer could refer to the job aid), then the content requires more explanation and standards that are less subjective (such as "delegated when possible"). The items on the Checklist are phrased poorly, and it would be difficult to determine if the project meets or does not meet those standards.

6. This Checklist reads as if it were more than a job aid; perhaps it is intended to serve as a quality control tool or a final step in submitting a project plan. If so, the job aid probably requires some space to indicate what plan/document it refers to, who the reviewer is, and the date of the review.

7. The job aid provides no before-and-after information to help the performer know what to expect before the step is completed and how to know if it has been successful.

Format-Specific Design Tips

Besides the general rules, there are tips that apply to specific job aid formats:

- *Reminder:* Keep Reminder job aids as simple as possible. Conciseness is critical. Being obvious or obtrusive is also important; placement of the job aid at the worksite is a key consideration.

- *Match:* The job aid should be as close to being identical to the comparison or product as possible.

- *Step:* Each step should be numbered. If space allows, each step should include information on before and after—what the performer should expect to see prior to taking the step and what it should look like after the step.

- *Checklist:* There should be a prominent box for entering a checkmark, the space for checks should be to the right of the step, and there should be a clear standard for a result so the user isn't confused about whether a checkmark is appropriate.

- *Worksheet:* Insert a completed example if space permits and provide designated, obvious spaces where information is to be entered. The Worksheet should include instructions on how to calculate answers. If space allows, it's also useful to show an incorrect calculation or a "wrong" example to compare with the correct sample.

- *Process Table or Flowchart:* Consider using symbols in the process to depict decision points, a process stimulus, and actions. At a minimum, use arrows to depict the direction as information or work proceeds through the process.

- *Decision Table:* Make sure the variables (the "ifs" and "thens") are clearly defined. No more than three "ifs" should lead to one "then." An "if" should never lead to more than one "then." Use horizontal arrows to indicate that the user should proceed to the next cell in the row. Place the entire job aid or the decision to be made within a box or some kind of border.

- *Troubleshooting Diagram:* Be sure to provide a clear path that is easy for the user to follow. Each step in the process should make it possible to rule out various possibilities, and each step should have at least two options (until the troubleshooting process can go no further). Also recognize that if a performer is consulting this job aid, it is likely that something has broken down or that problems have arisen, leading to job stress. Under stress, most humans experience poorer cognition and understanding; therefore, you should design job aids for such situations that are straightforward and as clear as possible.

▶ *Data Array:* Look for a method or scheme to organize the information in the job aid. The key factor is that the internal order should be logical to the user (for example, the most frequently requested phone numbers on top; in the sequence of the steps for an appeal process).

▶ *Script:* If some parts of the script are mandatory and other parts are only examples, make sure the script is obvious and explicit about which elements are mandatory. Use a contrasting color or boldface type for critical language. Also consider identifying the range of possible responses by the customer or client so the script allows users to see and anticipate the conversational flow.

Practice What You Learn

Here is another opportunity to apply what you've just learned about format-specific design rules.

The Scenario. Many professionals in the HR field have trouble deciding when ROI analysis is appropriate. You need to design a job aid that can help other trainers in your organization determine when they should or should not conduct an ROI analysis. Here is the content information that you have:

> It is appropriate to conduct an ROI analysis when a program is controversial and there is political opposition to it. You should also think about doing an ROI analysis if an initiative is resource intensive or expensive. If your budget is coming under scrutiny or if you need to justify your department's funding, then ROI can be helpful. You shouldn't plan on conducting an ROI analysis on programs that are somewhat similar if the first one has already been analyzed for the ROI. The exception would be if there was a need to choose between those two programs or compare them. Additionally, ROI is a useful tool for selecting among options when you have multiple programs but can only do one. ROI makes no sense when the intervention is required by law or is popular and enjoys organizational support. If the program is in the interim stages and is still going through formative evaluation, it would be premature to conduct an ROI analysis. And if the intervention is a one-time-only event, then an ROI analysis is likely to have little value (Phillips, 2003).

Your job is twofold: (1) decide which job aid format is appropriate for this task; and (2) create your own version of the job aid.

Expert Guidance. Because the purpose of the job aid is to help performers decide when an ROI analysis is appropriate, the appropriate format is a Decision Table. Job aid 5-1 shows a version of what this Decision Table might look like.

JOB AID 5-1. When to conduct an ROI analysis.

Trainers, performance consultants, and instructional designers should use this job aid to determine if an ROI (return-on-investment) analysis should be done.

If...	And...	Then...
If the initiative is controversial...	...others in the organization oppose it...	...conduct an ROI analysis.
If the initiative uses a lot of resources...	→	...conduct an ROI analysis.
If the initiative is required by law...	→	...skip an ROI analysis.
If the budget is under scrutiny or you're being asked to justify your department...	→	...conduct ROI analyses for key programs.
If there are several possible options to deal with a performance gap...	...you need to choose among the several options...	...conduct an ROI analysis to identify which intervention has the best return-on-investment.
If the initiative enjoys wide support...	...it is limited in scope or resources...	...skip the ROI analysis.
If the initiative is a one-time effort that will not be repeated...	→	...skip the ROI analysis.
If the initiative is still being refined and improved...	→	...don't do an ROI analysis until the formative evaluation is finished.
If the initiative is similar to another intervention that has already had an ROI analysis done...	→	...skip an ROI analysis unless there is a need to compare the two initiatives.

Functional Concerns

Because the job aid ultimately has to be functional in a work setting, there are other issues you'll want to consider during design. For instance, is the job aid durable? Something that looks great in the design studio needs to be developed with the understanding that it will get thrown in desk drawers, serve as a beverage coaster, double as a bookmark, and perhaps put in duty as a flyswatter. Electronic job aids, such as drop-down menus or pop-up screens, can run into problems when antivirus or security software scans the system to look for unexpected additions.

Relevant to this concern is the question of storage. Is this job aid likely to be stored with documentation or other job aids relevant to similar tasks? If so, then the job aid needs to be designed so it can be integrated and stored with similar items. As you look at the work environment and see how the performers use the job aid, you'll identify a host of other design considerations. For example, if the performer doesn't have an assigned workstation, as would be the case for someone who works in the field like a telephone lineman or emergency responder or field sales representative, and the job aid is designed to be used during the task, then it needs to be a job aid that is easily carried and very accessible

Figure 5-2 is an example of an intelligently designed job aid that accommodates functional and work setting demands. This job aid was created by the U.S. Department of Justice and the National Fire Academy. It was designed for first responders (fire, police, and emergency medical services) who are on-site for incidents potentially involving chemical, biological, or nuclear weapons. All first responders are likely to have had training on incidents involving weapons of mass destruction, but this is a classic case where a job aid makes sense: It involves memory of data rarely used (if at all) by the workers in question so the likelihood of memory lapse is great, such situations would likely involve high amounts of stress (so decision errors and recall mistakes would be likely), and the consequences of "getting it wrong" represent a life-or-death matter.

What makes this job aid so well-designed functionally? The job aid meets the following requirements:

- ▶ It is designed to fit in the pockets or vests of first responders or go into a police unit glove box. Remember, the performers don't have desks; if it isn't easy to carry, then they won't have it when they need it.
- ▶ It is spiral bound so in an emergency a first responder can tear out the relevant page and easily carry it or tape it to a vehicle console or tactical vest.

Figure 5-2. An example of designing for functional concerns.

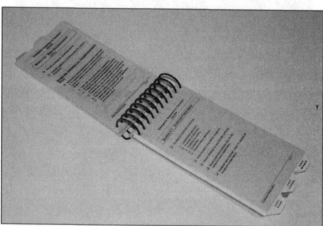

▶ It has stiff plastic pages. It can take dust, spilled coffee, and being tossed about. In addition, someone wearing gloves with a hazmat or biohazard suit would be able to flip the pages. The job aid is made from a plastic material that can handle a grease pencil, pen, or marker for on-site notes and reminders.

▶ The job aid has tabs and is color-coded, recognizing that first responders are likely to only need one of the several sections and must be able to find the relevant section quickly. Because of the stress of the situation, they aren't likely to refer to an index or table of contents to find the necessary information.

In sum, this job aid is an excellent example of one that has been designed with the exigencies of the work environment in mind.

Noted

As you design a job aid for a task that might already involve other types of material (other job aids or user manuals), consider how to integrate the job aid you're working on with the existing materials. That might include resizing your job aid, changing the template or fonts so they have a similar style, or producing a plastic pocket holder so your job aid can fit within a user manual stored at the worksite.

Working With an SME

When you develop a job aid, more than likely you'll spend some time working with an SME. Typically your first exposure with the SME will come during the task analysis phase (which happens prior to the design phase) of the job aid development process. However, you will likely involve the SME in the design and validation phases as well. Typically, you will garner input from the SME about the design, the accuracy of the job aid, the detail in the steps, and how functional the job aid is for the work environment.

There are five basic rules for dealing with an SME while developing a job aid:

1. Do your research up front. Before you talk to the SME, observe a performer first, talk to a manager, or read existing documentation for the job. Don't go into the initial SME interview unprepared as you'll miss opportunities to gain insight because of your ignorance about the work. You don't need to be an expert, but you need to know enough to be able to note some of the distinctions the SME makes. This initial knowledge also can help you spot instances when the SME inadvertently combines steps or leaves out details that have become internalized. Before you begin the design phase, start by reviewing your task analysis notes and rethink what you know about the work environment. Be sure to think about what kind of job aid the workers would use—not the kind of job aid you'd like to design.

2. Expect the process to be iterative. The task analysis, design, and validation phases of this process typically involve a lot of back and forth so that you

can learn about key parts of the task that have been internalized by the SME. Because of a phenomenon called unconscious competence, workers might perform a critical step without thinking about it. In these cases, you'll ask the SME to describe the steps involved, you'll document them, and then show the draft job aid to the SME who'll say, "You left out a step." You'll also find that some steps that workers insist on are actually preferences and are not critical to the task. You're likely to encounter similar glitches with the design of job aids. For example, you'll decide on a format (say, a Checklist) based on the SME's comments and run it by the SME who'll then reply, "Nah, the sequence is critical. You need to number those steps." A comment along such lines indicates that what's really needed is a Step job aid. Once you realize that the process is an iterative one, you won't become impatient or frustrated, plus you'll be able to set realistic expectations with the SME and the client.

3. Be careful of your assumptions. The world of the trainer or instructional designer is very different from the world of the frontline performer. Design elements that you find impressive might seem irrelevant or irritating to workers. Don't jump to conclusions. Test what you think you heard and confirm your understanding. When you get input on the design, probe a little deeper and challenge your conclusions. It's very easy for experienced designers to form an initial conclusion about things like what format to use or what the steps to the task are and then to ask confirming questions of the SME that only reinforce those initial assumptions.

4. Don't talk too much. Trainers tend to be persuasive people. If you're a trainer, you probably have good platform skills. It's too easy to dominate a meeting with an SME who is initially uncomfortable with the situation or not very talkative. When the SME initially seems to be hesitant or uncomfortable at elaborating, it's tempting for the trainer/designer to seek to fill the silence with his or her own words. Don't do it! During the task analysis, design, and validation phases, you want the SMEs and other feedback sources to talk. Sometimes silence will goad someone to talk. In any case, someone who is supposed to give you suggestions on the design can't give you input if you're the one doing the talking.

5. Leave your ego at the door. As a designer, it is natural for you to fall in love with your idea and the resulting design. You can't do that. As you develop

Noted

I learned a lesson about assumptions the hard way. I designed a job aid that consisted of a laminated pocket card for an organization located in the northeastern United States. I thought it was elegant and was very proud of my effort. Then, the client and I discovered that the employees were running through these job aids as if there was no tomorrow—completely exceeding our estimates of job aid replacement rates. The job aids were popular all right: Employees were using them as scrapers to remove ice from the windshields of their vehicles! I was guilty of not really understanding the work environment and assuming that what made sense for me in the southern United States would apply as well to my client's company.

the job aid, you need to be willing to let go of your idea. Yes, you shouldn't let the client dictate the design. Yes, you should stand up for positions dictated by the data. Nevertheless, there will be times in the design process when you like a particular format, a graphic image, the size of the job aid, or a media choice, but you'll get feedback during the validation along the lines of "Ugh—we'd never use that" or "I can't figure out how to access that menu!" or "This is just totally different from the other job aids in the series that we have to use." When you are getting design input from SMEs and potential users, you have to be open to their input even if it means discarding some of the design schemes you've fallen in love with. Additionally, it's only natural for you to take pride in your work. So, getting critical input during the design phase (and especially during the validation phase) can be hard to take. But you not only need to take it, you need to encourage it and use that input to create a better design.

Getting It Done

It is easy to get caught up in the desire to produce a job aid that you, as the designer, feel is elegant or has lots of bells and whistles. Your job is to reduce the complex (or difficult to do or hard to remember) into something that is simple. Don't get caught up in trying to be fancy with your design or create something that appeals only to you. Ultimately, the best test of how well designed your job aid is is the user's perception of it and the impact it has on closing the performance gap.

Remember this as you have another chance in exercise 5-1 to practice applying what you learned about job aid design in this chapter.

Exercise 5-1. Revisiting job aid design.

1. Working effectively with SMEs is critical for the task analysis, design, and validation phases of the job aid development process. Think about the culture of your company or of your most consistent client. What is it about the culture and background of the workforce that complicates working with SMEs on something like a job aid project? For instance, is there a perception in the field that support functions (like training) or representatives from headquarters don't know what work on the line is like? What could you do to overcome or minimize these barriers?

2. Find an example of a job aid you encounter at work. Using the standards or rules in this chapter, critique it. In what ways could you improve that job aid?

3. Design a job aid of your own. Follow the development process laid out in chapter 4 and the design rules covered in this chapter.

4. Not all job aids follow the design rules laid out in this chapter. Oftentimes, the designer is forced to choose between two rules, such as providing sufficient white space versus explaining what happens before and after each step. Identify one of the job aids provided in this book that doesn't follow some of the design rules and determine for yourself if you feel there were acceptable reasons for breaking the rules.

5. Think of the format-specific guidelines provided in this chapter. What other rules or guidelines would you add that are specific to particular job aid formats?

This chapter has given you a chance to practice designing your own job aids. If you found some of the design work to be difficult, remember two things: First, task analysis data drives the design process; and second, the more you practice designing job aids, the better you'll get. The next chapter looks at validation and implementation.

6

Testing and
Implementation

■ ■

What's Inside This Chapter

Here you'll learn:

▶ How to do a formative evaluation of your job aid to
improve it
▶ Key factors to consider for a successful rollout of a job aid
▶ How to improve acceptance and garner buy-in for the job aid.

Formative Evaluation

You've done your analysis and you've designed a job aid. Now comes the time to get
feedback on the initial draft and build in improvements. This constitutes the validation and troubleshooting phases. This is also what is called formative evaluation.

Formative evaluation is the process of identifying ways to improve the design
and checking feedback on the job aid. It is critical to do a formative evaluation with
any job aid you design. No matter how confident you are with the initial design, a
job aid prototype always benefits from validation and troubleshooting. This is

because the test of how good a job aid is is not based on your comfort level with the design, it's based on the users' reactions and how well the job aid fits the work circumstances. This is the time when you involve the users and seek their input in regard to the initial design.

Basic Rule 9

Always test the initial design of a job aid. You must confirm how well the design fits the users' needs and work demands.

To validate the design, you test the job aid prototype and get input from potential users. There are a number of factors involved in testing the job aid prototype and getting feedback. Specifically, you need to validate three elements of the job aid: accuracy, usability, and alignment.

Job Aid Accuracy

Accuracy looks at the content of the job aid. An accurate job aid is one that is technically correct; there are no factual or functional mistakes. Although all elements of the validation focus are important, this is the most critical. If your job aid isn't usable, than it will be a wasted effort. If your job aid isn't aligned, then it won't solve the problem. If it is inaccurate, you will produce failure by having performers follow advice that is wrong or incomplete and could also generate legal or liability issues. As a result, job aid accuracy is incredibly important—it all starts with being sure that the job aid content does indeed describe the task correctly.

Surprisingly, achieving accuracy with the job aid isn't as easy as you'd think. Oftentimes, the translation from SME to designer (and then conversion to job aid prototype) leads to errors or gaps in the content. Sometimes an SME unintentionally describes a job process incompletely or incorrectly. Remember, an SME is a good performer because of the ability to get the work done. It is a rare SME who can also explain the work process clearly, concisely, and explicitly.

You will often discover that an initial task analysis that you and the SME are happy with is incorrect because of the SME's inability to explain how the work is actually done and the steps that are really part of that task. Oftentimes, these lapses occur because the SME or key performer is an unconscious performer; he or she just isn't aware of the critical steps of the work because the SME or key performers do them naturally and automatically. In any case, it's critical to confirm the accuracy of the job aid. Unfortunately, accuracy is a frequent problem because of the difficulty of precisely identifying what is and is not part of the task that the job aid seeks to address.

Think About This

Once you've developed a job aid prototype, plan on showing it to a different key performer or expert from the one in your original task analysis. You might discover that a new set of eyes can identify gaps or inaccurate steps that the original creators failed to see.

Generally speaking, there are several issues you'll want to consider when you validate the accuracy of the job aid. First, is it *technically* correct? Is there any way that a worker or professional could argue that the content is factually wrong? Second, is the job aid *functionally* correct? Job aid content can be correct technically but fail to acknowledge some of the practical realities of the job. The question of functional accuracy gets at whether the content is accurate in regard to how the job is actually done (rather than what the policy and procedure manual states). Recognize that sometimes there might be an internal conflict between the technical and functional accuracy; you'll need to resolve that conflict by pushing management to resolve it. Additionally, you'll check for completeness: Are there any gaps in the process? Sometimes what is on the job aid is accurate—as far as it goes—but it doesn't go far enough or is incomplete.

Job Aid Usability

Usability in the validation and troubleshooting phases involves determining if the job aid is workable and user friendly. If you have done a good job on the task analysis, you are likely to find only minor problems in this area. However, absent a job aid that scores well in the usability column, you will have spent valuable time and resources on a piece of work that only collects dust.

One element of usability involves language. Obviously you check for correct spelling and grammar. You'll want to make sure that the language and use of terms are consistent. Are abbreviations explained in the job aid? Is the language appropriate not only for the performer, but also for the work setting? For instance, high-stress situations or ones in which the job aid is to be used during the task call for a much simpler and direct use of language. This may mean composing in key phrases rather than in sentences. Ultimately, the biggest test for language and usability is clarity: How clear is the job aid?

You can identify usability concerns through a variety of tests. Some language issues can be handled individually by the designer or by showing the job aid to a new set of eyes or by turning to a professional editor. It's certainly possible to show the job aid to a performer and ask for feedback about how easy or difficult it will be to use at work. However, the best usability testing involves giving the job aid to performers and observing their use and application (or misuse and misapplication) of the job aid. A close second would be to have the performers use the job aid and then report back, often using a feedback form you've designed, to collect this data. The key point from both of these methods is this: *Nothing beats usability testing that involves actually giving the job aid to users and having them use it at work.*

It is important to understand that people change their behavior when they know they're being observed. When you give a job aid to a worker, you can't assume the

Basic Rule 10
The best form of usability testing is to give the job aid prototype to actual performers to see how they do with it.

Noted

Don't deploy a job aid without doing validation unless it is an absolute emergency. No matter how good a job aid looks after the first draft, without user testing and refinement, you will be deploying a flawed product. The only justification for rolling out a job aid without seeking feedback first and revising it is if you face an emergency so great that the consequences of not correcting the performance are far greater than the impact of mistakes that could be caused by the job aid.

performer's behavior is natural. Performer feedback in an artificial setting has some value, but you also need to find out how naturally the worker turns to the job aid or how easily it is integrated into the task. For that kind of insight, you need to create as natural a work setting as possible. Try to have the performer actually use the job aid at work (rather than pulling the worker away from the job to provide feedback). Look for ways to minimize your presence during the data collection process. It may be preferable to give the worker the job aid, walk away, and then collect feedback after the task has been performed by debriefing the performer.

Basic Rule 11

When you observe the performer using the job aid, do not help the worker with the job aid. Any struggles the user has provide invaluable data for you and your redesign of the initial prototype.

When you are observing the worker use the job aid, there are several critical things to keep in mind. First, do not help the worker use the job aid. If the performer encounters difficulty or confusion, do not help him or her through the problems. You not only need to see what problems arise, but also how the performer overcomes (if possible) those barriers. If the job aid isn't user friendly, you need to be able to observe this (as well as just how much of a barrier this is to any potential use). Answering questions or showing the user how it works defeats the point of this step. Do not rationalize the need to coach the user by arguing that unless the worker can open the help menu or decode the format you can't evaluate other aspects of the job aid. If the worker can't figure out how to use it, you need to see how much frustration the user will tolerate before discarding or ignoring the job aid. Second, always intervene if the worker is about to make a dangerous or costly mistake. Your job aid trial should not result in people being placed in danger or damage to work. Stop the job aid trial if either appears likely to occur.

Basic Rule 12

Always intervene if it appears that the trial of the job aid could result in a costly error or potential danger.

As you observe or debrief a performer, it is important to take notes during the trial or the debriefing. Do not plan on observing the user and jotting down your thoughts and observations after it is all over. One of the more common errors with observation of the demonstration is the failure to completely and accurately capture information, either through your observation or feedback provided by the user. It's often a good idea to have a copy of the job aid with you as you observe the performer, assuming the job aid is a text-based document you can produce a paper copy of. That way you can jot down notes and observations directly on the job aid.

Be sure to arrange participants for usability trials before you start the design phase and certainly before you get to the validation phase. As a designer, it is easy to assume that you won't have trouble getting volunteers to try using the job aid. But, if you wait until after the first prototype is nearly finished to set up the trial and seek volunteer testers, you'll delay the project significantly. You'll almost always discover that everyone is in the middle of other work and it isn't convenient for them to test your job aid draft. Consequently, you can add weeks to your project delivery by waiting until the last minute to pick testers and arrange the validation protocol. Do this work up front before you've begun the actual design so volunteers or assigned testers know to expect this commitment and can prepare for it.

Sometimes it's not possible to actually observe performers use the job aid. That may be because much of the work is cognitive and observation may not tell you what is going through the worker's head. Or, the work occurs in the field or in locations where an observer isn't permitted. In those cases, you may want to consider providing a feedback form to be sure that performers are accurate and complete in the feedback they provide. This means it is critical for you to anticipate issues you want their reactions to and then design a feedback form that encourages a systematic approach instead of just asking for summary reactions.

It's a good idea to provide a form for SMEs who are testing the job aid draft. Figure 6-1 is an example of a combination Step-Worksheet job aid developed to capture input for performers. Even though there are no calculations necessary, the worksheet helps channel user feedback into a particular format, making it easier for the designer to use that input. In this instance, the reviewers were examining a series of help screens and pull-down menus that had been added to a database to remind users of a series of functions. You'll notice how the job aid lays out the steps necessary to use the job aid. It also includes a "thank you" reminder directed to the reviewers. No matter how willing individuals are initially to serve as reviewers, when the time comes for their input, it is always a good idea for you to make it clear that you're grateful for their help with this project.

Figure 6-1. Example of a feedback and review form.

Use this form to capture your comments as you review the help screens for the new database upgrade.

1. Put your name and the date in the spaces provided at the top of the form.
2. Put the screen number (located in the upper right hand corner) on the form for each pull-down menu or help screen you use.
3. Write down any problems, confusing elements, or reactions to any part of the help screen. **Important: Please write down your comments as you use the screen. Do not wait until after you've finished using the program.**
4. Add any suggestions in the last column.
5. Submit your Feedback and Review form by Friday at 4 p.m. to the IT department by interoffice mail or email.

Thank you again for your help with this project.

Reviewer: _____   Date: _____

Screen #	Reactions to or Problems With the Screen	Suggestions or Improvements

For usability testing, in particular, you'll need to do some thinking about which users you want to get feedback from. It is tempting to sign up the first warm bodies who volunteer to help with the validation testing. It is true that sometimes you'll struggle to get anyone at all to review the job aid draft. Nevertheless, it's critical for you to get the right reviewers. At a minimum, you should look for a fresh set of eyes (someone different from the original SME used in your task analysis) who will be called upon to use the job aid at work (rather than another trainer).

Technology-based job aids require even more thought as to user feedback. For instance, with an EPSS or technology-based job aid, you should identify a combination of users, including a novice user (who is uncomfortable or inexperienced with the software or system), a power user (who knows the technology well but is not necessarily an expert at the task), an SME (who is an expert at the task and perhaps a key performer or exemplar), and an IT or systems representative (who might discover problems, not with the individual use of the job aid, but how it must be integrated into the technology or maintained by the system). This range of testers for technology-based job aids is because even simple job aids (such as a pull-down menu or initial information screen) usually has a wider range of potential "fit" issues to be sure it works both for the universe of possible performers and within the technology systems.

Job Aid Alignment

Alignment is the third element that you check during the validation phase. Alignment assesses whether the job aid addresses or is used to deal with the performance gap or task originally identified. If you've done a good job on the task analysis, alignment is not likely to be a significant problem. Nevertheless, this does not mean that you can skip this part of the validation phase.

It is not uncommon to discover that workers are using your job aid in a manner you did not anticipate. For instance, a laminated pocket card might become a bookmark, a letter opener or an ice remover. A compact disk full of job aids and help menus serves as a drink coaster instead. Although those are somewhat extreme examples, more typical instances involve situations where the job aid is appropriate for a particular task but not the task it was originally designed for. For example, a sales closing job aid on how to answer customer objections might have ended up as a job aid that provides reminders for potential buyers about program benefits. Because the focus of the job aid has changed (probably accidentally), the original performance problem (low sale close rates because of weak responses to customer objections) hasn't been addressed. Another instance might be where instead of using a job aid to reinforce performance on the job, it is given out at new employee orientation as a means to reduce training time. But, the end result is that existing performers don't receive the new job aid and the new performers never get the chance to build the skills that allow the job aid to be effective. Therefore, it is important to reexamine the original justification for the job aid, the task or performance gap that was supposed to be addressed, and what the job aid actually ends up being used for.

Think About This

Alignment problems can happen easily with job aids. Sometimes this is a function of poor focus on the design end. It may be a result of user confusion as to the job aid's purpose. A clear title and initial explanation at the top of the job aid can often eliminate many alignment problems that are a result of the performer using the job aid for the wrong task. If workers are intentionally using job aids for purposes they were not intended for, such alignment problems can only be solved by a good understanding of the work environment so that the job aid is not susceptible to misuse.

Part of the challenge in assessing alignment is that workers may hide how they are misusing the job aid. Or, perhaps it is not obvious that the job aid is being misapplied. For instance, consider the example mentioned earlier of a job aid designed to improve a sales close rate by providing answers to common customer objections. You might observe the sales rep during a client meeting and see the sales rep refer to the job aid during the sales close. But, because the employee is using the job aid to talk about benefits of the product (and not to counter customer objections), it ends up being misapplied and the sales closing problem isn't solved. Although you would see the job aid referred to and the content used in the sales pitch, unless you listened carefully and knew the sales task well enough, you wouldn't realize that the job aid had been applied incorrectly. This also illustrates how, if you had to depend solely upon feedback by the performer, you'd likely miss this issue because the user isn't likely to be aware that the job aid is being used inappropriately.

The alignment assessment usually requires perceptiveness on the part of the designer. You need to determine if the job aid was used correctly and used for the proper task. You'll also need to judge whether the job aid is being misused covertly. In some instances, the way to obtain this information does not come from observing the worker with the job aid but by checking it after the workday is complete. For instance, are there strange stains or wear patterns on the job aid? Are job aids ending up in locations away from the worksite or with employees who don't do that task? Is the workforce running through the job aids at a faster rate than you expected? Should any of these scenarios be true, it's not necessarily a negative consideration. Perhaps the job aid is more useful or needed across a broader spectrum than you and the client anticipated. You just won't know that until you assess for alignment.

Building in Improvements

After you've tested the job aid design, you'll need to incorporate the feedback into the design and make changes. This should be followed with another set of testing and user feedback. Sometimes you'll discover that feedback you received, despite being well-intentioned, is erroneous. Thus, the validation and troubleshooting phases of the job aid development process might involve some repetition as you work to get everything right.

Rollout

You've got a job aid you feel good about, and you've validated the design with a series of user tests and editing reviews. You've made a few modest changes based on the user input, and it looks like the job aid is ready to go. What now? You can't just start handing it out to workers—or can you? Rollout and implementation strategies vary tremendously depending upon the workforce and nature of the job aid.

For starters, you may have to provide some kind of training to workers on how to use this job aid. As discussed in chapter 4, the third phase of the job aid development process is to determine if your job aid will require training and, if so, just how much and what kind. It is extremely rare that a job aid can simply be distributed to the workforce with no preamble or advance setup and preparation. Many designers take the perspective that their role is to create the job aid and once that's done, their role is over. Nothing could be further from the truth. Absent intelligent planning about rollout, the job aid will end up being misused or ignored by those it's intended to benefit.

The choice of rollout and implementation strategies depends upon many different variables. There is no standard approach for implementing a new job aid. Here are some of the questions that you need to answer to determine how to best implement a new job aid:

- How widespread are the potential users? Is this job aid for a limited pool of performers (such as a team or one category of employees like administrative assistants), or will it be distributed across the workforce?
- Does the job aid require some sort of training or orientation? If so, how extensive? Does this training require practice and role plays?
- Is this a new job aid or a replacement of an existing one? If it's a replacement, is it simply updated information, or does it call for workers to use the job aid in a different manner (such as moving from a paper copy to a PDA-based aid)? What will be done with the old job aids? Is there a negative result (such as incorrect work) if performers continue to use the old job aid in preference over the new version?
- Is the workforce used to relying on job aids or will this be a new experience for them? Is the job aid to be integrated into an existing family of job aids (so it's consistent in look and feel to other products the workforce uses)?
- Was the trigger for this job aid initiated by demands from the workers? Does the workforce have any idea that the job aid is coming? How enthusiastic do performers seem to be about the job aid? What did the user tests tell you about acceptance and buy-in?
- What is the nature of the workforce? Are the workers centralized or spread out? Is there shift work or a strong reliance on part-time, seasonal, field-based, or co-located employees?
- What did your task analysis and validation phases show to be the biggest barriers to effective use of the job aid? What kinds of resistance (intentional or unconscious) will you need to overcome? In what ways will employees need to change how they do things if they are to use the job aid appropriately?
- Is there likely to be any embarrassment associated with using the job aid? Will there be peer pressure to avoid using the job aid?
- Is the job aid to be stand-alone, integrated, or embedded? If it's going to be integrated or stand-alone, what storage provisions need to be made (such as applying Velcro tape to all computer monitors to attach the job aid or making sure all employees have a place to put the laminated sheet or CD)? If it is

to be attached to another piece of equipment (a dashboard or computer or ladder), is there another department that "owns" that tool? If so, do you need their agreement before you can attach the job aid?

▶ Does frontline management know about this? If employees come up with questions, will these managers be able to answer them? Will they be advocates for the job aid?

▶ Are there any incentives for employees to use the job aid? What happens to the worker who doesn't use it?

Noted

The key point to understand about any rollout initiative is that just because the job aid is self-explanatory doesn't mean implementation planning is not necessary. Even if a job aid is simple and straightforward, performers might push back if they showed up for work one day and found it attached to their computer screens. Or, management might feel that corporate headquarters was meddling. Rollout issues are affected by the nature of the workforce, habits, organizational culture, and experience with other job aids. The rollout might be very simple (people come to work the next day to discover the job aid on their desks with a short note) or very complex and involved. Do not assume that the extent and type of implementation planning should be based solely upon how clear and intuitive the job aid is.

Acceptance and Buy-in

You need to focus on acceptance and buy-in from several different levels. At the front end of the project, there is the issue of management support for the job aid process. You might face managers who want to buy new toys or spend a lot on training instead of going with a far more efficient job aid. You might have clients who attempt to short-circuit the process. They could argue there is no need for a task analysis or validation phase. Finally, there is the acceptance of the users themselves. It might be necessary to overcome user resistance to using the job aid. How can you do this?

Start by selling the job aid to the highest level in the organization that you can. The person who contacts you about this work is your client, but you want to go above your client for more background and support. As a rule of thumb, where your client is organizationally, go at least two levels higher. Ideally you should go as high as you can in the organizational structure.

Once you start talking to people about the job aid, focus on performance. Talk about the current performance gap and what it's costing the organization. Describe the performance the job aid is to focus on. Job aids usually have a very high ROI ratio, especially in comparison to many other interventions such as training or organization development activities or equipment/resource acquisitions. Comparing potential ROI across a body of options is a very compelling way of generating support for job aids as well as boosting your perceived value within the organization.

On occasion, you might get some pushback from clients about the job aid development process. Some clients might argue that there is no need for a task analysis or validation or even rollout. You will probably find that it is easier to sell clients on the needs for those phases not by arguing they're critical for a well-designed job aid, but by talking about them in terms of potential resistance and buy-in. Don't tell management you need to talk to an SME to design it correctly because management is probably already sure they know what it needs to look like. Argue that by talking to an SME and involving the workers, they will be happier with the result and more likely to accept it. Most managers can probably think of plenty of times when resistance and the lack of buy-in were deadly. Therefore, referring to those issues is likely to be more persuasive than trying to sell them on the integrity of the process.

Basic Rule 13

Involve the union at the earliest possible stage of the job aid development process.

Besides going as high as you can organizationally, there are others in the organization who could help build acceptance and even generate excitement for the job aid. If the client organization is unionized, be sure to include the local union representative at the earliest possible opportunity. You can't afford to make the union an enemy when it comes to job aids; employees simply have too much discretion about when to use or not use a job aid. If the union passes down a negative word, your job aid will not be used.

Conversely, if the union becomes an enthusiastic proponent of your job aid, you probably don't even need official management support; bootleg copies would magically find their way to the shop floor and mysteriously reproduce themselves. Additionally, it's ideal if the SME you get involved in the task analysis also happens to be highly regarded or well-respected within the workforce. Having someone on board whom other workers look up to goes a long way to gaining support for the job aid.

Basic Rule 14

If you have a choice, pick an SME for your task analysis and validation phases who is well-respected and looked up to by co-workers.

ROI analysis is almost always a major selling point for any job aid, especially with management. Simply put, a job aid usually is substantially less expensive than most other possible solutions. In securing support for your job aid, remember to sell to the interests of the particular person or group you're dealing with. Consequently, a key performer might initially have little interest in cooperating for a task that qualifies as extra work. Supervisors might throw up many barriers, being reluctant to let you borrow a top performer and uncertain about changing how work is done. Performers might perceive this as a cut-rate solution or believe they already know how to do the work. Management might have notions about what will solve the problem or how to go about creating the job aid.

You need to look at what drives the interests of each party. For management, it might be ROI and a quick solution. For supervisors, it might be less worker downtime than training or the ability to couple the job aid with another supervisor priority. For performers, it might be making work easier. For an SME, it might be pride in work or an appeal to expertise.

In all instances, the client needs to own responsibility for the use of the job aid. As a designer, you can't control whether the job aid is used by workers (or if supervisors support or discourage use). You can design the job aid to make it as easy as possible to use. You can create a rollout plan that enhances the likelihood of use. Regardless, the client still has to own this issue. Otherwise, the client will focus on other, more exciting issues and the job aid will drop by the wayside.

How can you keep the client responsible for usage of the job aid? Part of this is in managing expectations from the very beginning of the job aid development process. You need to continually remind clients that the problem isn't solved as soon as the job aid is created. There needs to be a roll-out process, workers need to use the job aid, and then it needs to be supported and maintained.

You can focus this responsibility through measurement. What gets measured gets done. As the designer, you're likely to be held accountable (and evaluated) on whether the job aid is created. Push to have someone else accountable for the degree to which it is used. Additionally, evaluate the success of the job aid. Measure how much impact the job aid had in reduction of the performance gap. In conducting this evaluation, you inevitably get into looking at usage because you need to determine the degree of usage to assess how much impact the job aid is responsible for.

Getting It Done

Now that you've learned more about improving job aid designs and getting buy-in, you'll have an opportunity to put some of this information to practice. Exercise 6-1 offers some things you can do that will give you a chance to apply what you learned in this chapter.

Exercise 6-1. Thinking about testing and implementation of job aids.

1. How could you identify a potential SME who also has a great deal of respect from co-workers?

2. Examine the job aid you developed in chapter 5. What would an appropriate validation process look like for the job aid? How would you collect the user input? What potential problems do you anticipate with the first draft?

3. How could you sell this job aid to management? What are possible barriers to use or acceptance that you anticipate with this job aid?

(continued on page 116)

4. Given what you know about your client, what would an effective roll-out process look like for your job aid?

5. Can you think of any instances where it might make sense to have a "stealth" rollout with minimal publicity or advance discussion before job aids are disseminated to workers?

In the upcoming chapter, you'll get a chance to look at evaluation as a means of measuring the success of your job aid in closing a performance gap.

7

Evaluating Job Aids

....

What's Inside This Chapter

Here you'll learn:

▶ How to evaluate the organizational and performance impacts of job aids
▶ Why evaluation is a critical aspect of job aid design
▶ Ways to evaluate bundled job aids
▶ Measuring return-on-expectations.

Evaluating Results

There is a tendency to shortchange evaluation and ignore its importance. In some cases, the client is in a hurry and doesn't have the patience to come back and evaluate the results. In other cases, the consultant or designer believes that evaluation is too difficult or—for some soft-skill issues—impossible to measure. Both perspectives are wrong and shortsighted. Evaluation is important for many reasons.

For starters, you need to evaluate the job aid to determine the kinds of improvements required, especially if you have a client who resists evaluating. One approach for dealing with clients who push back when you speak of evaluation is instead to talk in terms of "next steps" or "refining the prototype." Oftentimes a client who bristles at the idea of evaluation easily acquiesces to the concept of determining what comes next in the path to continuous improvement—and that is part of what evaluation is all about—determining what progress has been made, how to make it better, and what should happen next. Evaluation is necessary so you can generate a job aid that does what it is supposed to do. Even if the client sees little value in evaluating the job aid, evaluation is something that you need to find a way to make happen.

Basic Rule 15

Take the time to evaluate your job aids. You need to do this to improve the design, demonstrate effectiveness, and show that job aids can be a superior approach to many other options that management might push.

Summative Evaluation

At this point, it's helpful to do a quick review of terms. In the previous chapter you learned about formative evaluation. Formative evaluation assesses how well designed an intervention is. A formative evaluation of a job aid would seek ways to improve the design. In contrast, summative evaluation looks at the impact—especially in terms of performance and organizational results—of an intervention. Once you've deployed your job aid, you'll probably want to do some form of summative evaluation to assess how successful the job aid was in reducing performance problems.

You might hear people argue that it's too difficult or impossible to conduct a summative evaluation that measures the impact of job aids, especially ones dealing with soft skills. That is nonsense! Evaluation of job aids, even ones that are bundled with other solutions or involve soft skills, is very doable. Assessing the job aid's impact on worker performance goes to the very heart of why the job aid was designed. Why create the job aid if you aren't interested in determining if worker performance is improved? Assessing the organizational impact is actually very easy in many instances. Furthermore, because job aids typically have high ROIs, it makes sense for you to evaluate the success of your job aid efforts for political purposes.

Noted

Job aids are usually much less expensive than many other interventions, such as classes, team-building, process redesigns, job restructuring, or coaching programs, yet they can often be just as effective. Therefore, job aids are capable of achieving astronomically high ROI ratios. It is worth your time to make the effort at determining the ROI for some of your job aid projects.

Planning for Evaluation

The first thing to understand about evaluating job aids is that if your job aid initiative started out with a legitimate trigger (such as a front-end analysis, conversion of training content or training support), then measuring the impact of the job aid is significantly easier. If there is no legitimate trigger and the initiative was started because a job aid "just seemed like a good idea," or "because management insisted on it," then evaluation becomes much more difficult.

The trigger provides a clear target to aim for. This matters because the evaluation process actually starts before any job aid has ever been designed or distributed. Effective evaluation demands that you determine what the critical targets are that the organization seeks to improve. These targets can be either organizational goals or performance results. In either case, you have something to provide direction and also a baseline or goal to measure progress against.

For instance, suppose that you've been directed to develop a job aid as a means of shortening an existing training course. The training department's task analysis has shown than some of the activities in the course can be replaced by job aids. The purpose for doing this is to shorten the technical training course from 10 days to seven days. Because you're clear on the trigger for this process (shortening the length of the course by replacing some of the practice exercises with job aids), you now have something to measure against. You could determine if using the job aids does indeed reduce the length of the course (without reducing performance), and you could calculate the savings produced by shortening the course (and producing effective workers quicker). This is possible because the trigger to the job aid process provided a goal for tracking progress and a result to measure the impact of the job aid against.

Noted

The rationale for beginning a job aid project is critical not only because it determines if the project is legitimate, but also because it shapes how easy evaluation will be for you. A job aid initiated on a whim or without a clear focus will be much more subjective, and it will be harder to measure the ultimate impact on the organization or performer.

Related to this point is the importance of a task analysis. If there is no task analysis done as part of the job aid development process (or if the task analysis is shoddy and sloppy), then it is extremely difficult to isolate the skills and steps you are evaluating, unnecessarily complicating the evaluation process. A strong task analysis makes it possible for your evaluation to target particular skills (or steps) to measure and reliably assume that the job aid focuses on that specific performance issue. Additionally, the task analysis may have identified the impact of particular steps (or the degree to which some steps are critical to the overall task result), which also helps the evaluation process.

In any case, it is important to recognize that actions you take (or don't take) at the beginning of the process—the trigger that starts work on the job aid and the task analysis within the development process—can make your evaluation of the results much easier (or harder).

The Five Levels of Evaluation

One typology for training evaluation was developed by Donald Kirkpatrick (1975). Kirkpatrick's approach has four levels of evaluation:

- ▸ reaction
- ▸ learning
- ▸ application on the job
- ▸ business results.

Level 1 or reaction deals with participant or user comments. Level 1 evaluation is very valuable for the formative evaluation process. Designers typically rely heavily on performer feedback with initial prototypes, and this is a form of level 1 evaluation.

Level 1 data, however, is not likely to be your best source of data for overall results: You aren't usually as interested in whether performers like the job aid. Instead, you'll want to know what impact it had on the organization or the performance gap.

Level 2 deals measures the degree of learning or skills acquired. This is likely to be less relevant for you as a job aid designer. Remember, job aids are not a substitute for training; they do not teach new skills. A job aid can be used within a course to build confidence in a set of new skills or to enhance memory or reinforce what performers have learned. Consequently, there may be times when you as a designer will do a level 2 evaluation of a job aid. However, in these instances it will be difficult (but not impossible) to separate the impact of the job aid from the impacts of other interventions (such as the initial skills training).

Level 3 measures performance on the job. Level 3 involves a determination of whether performers have changed how they do the work and what results they get. Are employees doing better work? Has the performance gap been closed? Regardless of what kind of evaluation you do, you will usually plan on evaluating at level 3. It isn't very helpful if workers like the job aid or remember key material presented by the job aid but there is no change in performance. The purpose of the job aid is to improve performance. Therefore, a level 3 evaluation is the most common type of evaluation you'll need to conduct for most job aid assessments. You could choose to evaluate other elements of the job aid, but, from the beginning, you should give thought to how you will track the change in performance on the job.

Level 4 focuses on business results. In this case, you're determining whether sales went up, customer retention improved, costs decreased, or rework was minimized. The higher in the organization your client is, the more likely it is that your client will want you to demonstrate an impact on the business. Although level 4 evaluation is generally regarded as very forbidding to many designers and trainers, the real key to a comparatively easy level 4 evaluation process is to begin evaluation at the start of the design process. If you have a clear, legitimate trigger to start the entire job aid design process (such as a demonstrated performance gap or a critical business need), then you will have a target to measure against.

To Kirkpatrick's four levels of evaluation, we can add what has been referred to by Jack Phillips (2003) and others as level 5, or ROI. The distinction between Kirkpatrick's level 4 and Phillips's level 5 is that level 4 looks at whether or not organizational goals were met and level 5 assesses whether those goals were worth achieving. Stated otherwise, sometimes it may cost an organization so much to achieve a goal that it cost more than it gained. For instance, you could create a job aid to remind a fleet of truck drivers to periodically check their temperature gauges because the model of truck they are driving has a tendency to overheat, but using the job aid leads to an increase in accidents on the road, which more than outweighs the possible benefits of detecting the overheated engine early. ROI is an especially valuable measure for job aids because you may often discover that a job aid doesn't get the best business result as another intervention, but because of the significantly lower cost may end up with a much higher ROI.

Isolating the Impact

A common refrain from many designers and trainers (and one that is used to try and justify why evaluation beyond level 1 is futile) is that it is impossible or too difficult to measure the impact of a job aid given the range of other factors in play on the job. Nothing could be further from the truth: Evaluation is much easier than most trainers recognize.

If the job aid design is triggered by a front-end analysis or root-cause assessment, then evaluating the resulting impact is comparatively straightforward. The data from the front-end analysis allows you to distinguish the impact. If you've conducted a thorough task analysis and you're confident in your data, then that task analysis usually allows you to determine how much impact a particular step has in achieving a particular result.

A wide range of methods can be used to isolate the impact of an intervention on the job site, as Phillips (2003) notes. One of the more obvious ones available to most trainers is to utilize a control population. You're not likely to be able to disseminate the job aid to all workers simultaneously. Use this logistical constraint to your advantage because the phased dissemination of the job aid creates natural control groups. Provide the job aid to one shift or location first, and then compare results with groups that haven't gotten the job aid yet.

Deciding What to Evaluate

As mentioned earlier, your task analysis will have highlighted a particular task or set of steps that the performer needs assistance with. Here's an example to help clarify this concept. Imagine that the managers in the records department have complained about how long it takes to complete a request to provide a customer purchase record (such as when the sales department wants to see a buyer's history with the company or if the service department needs to verify a customer purchase and review history before authorizing a return). Since the implementation of the new database system, it takes significantly longer for the records staff to complete a request to provide a record on a specific customer or transaction. The managers want the record request cycle to be 30 percent shorter, from an average of 10 minutes down to seven minutes.

Your task analysis identifies the steps involved in this job—from the initial request received by the records clerk to the point that the customer record is provided to the employee who requested it. You discover that when too many computer screens are open at one time, the system tends to crash and all the entered data is lost, forcing the records clerk to start over. The clerks have been trained that the old computers can barely handle the new database system so they should avoid having many screens open or the system will crash. But, the clerks get caught up in the work and forget about the number of open screens.

You design a job aid with the help of the IT department. When either the system is close to crashing (because of the memory used) or when the number of screens open exceeds a safe number, the software will flash a warning on the monitor to close some screens or risk a crash. The validation and troubleshooting phases demonstrate that this reminder inserted into the software works.

How could you evaluate the success of your job aid? You've got a number of options. For starters, you should be able to observe a number of performers during the validation phase to determine how much faster the record request cycle is and then generalize that to the rest of the record clerks. Or, you could ask a sample of performers to record the number of crashes before and after the introduction of the job aid. If you identify what a typical computer crash costs in terms of time, you could extrapolate to the entire department. In either case, you could document how much shorter the record request cycle is (and how close it is to seven minutes).

If the organization can demonstrate that a shorter record request cycle has an impact on such measures as customer satisfaction, sales volume, costs associated with record retrieval, and costs passed onto the company because of the lag in returns, then quantifying the ROI for the job aid would be straightforward. It shouldn't be difficult to compare the ROI for the job aid with alternatives that were considered by managers (such as retraining all of the records clerks or replacing all of the computers). Slightly more challenging measures would involve asking managers or performers after the job aid has been rolled out to identify improvements and whether they're due to the job aid.

Noted

Evaluating the impact of a job aid isn't difficult, but the key to evaluation starts at the begin-ning of the process. You need to identify either organizational targets (through the front-end analysis) or key skills and tasks (through the task analysis) prior to the start or at the beginning of the development process. Those not only provide targets to aim for, but also focus on some-thing that matters to the organization (achieving a particular result or completing a task) and they also provide something specific to measure against. The trigger for the job aid design process can be critical in identifying what to focus on.

Evaluating Bundled Job Aids

Sometimes job aids are part of a larger package. Examples would include a combina-tion of training, coaching, process improvement, and job aids as support. How can you evaluate the impact of a job aid when there are so many confounding variables?

Although the integrated nature of the job aid does make it difficult to isolate the impact from the job aid, it isn't as difficult as it might first seem. It is rare that all interventions occur simultaneously; more often, the various solutions are phased in at different points. Because of resource constraints (not enough trainers, can't take everyone out of the call center at the same time to participate in the team-building session), it is rare that a multiple-intervention project calls for implementing every-thing simultaneously.

Additionally, it usually isn't feasible to provide everyone the job aid at the same time. For various reasons, one location gets the job aid before the other regions. This is often due to the limited resources available to disseminate the job aid. You might be the only one available to orient employees and disseminate copies even though there are eight locations in the organization.

Staggered rollouts offer an important advantage for evaluation, however: You have an automatic control population available. You can compare one shift or loca-tion (with the job aid) versus the results of a second shift or location (that hasn't received the job aid yet).

Return-on-Expectations

One evaluation approach that can be especially useful for evaluating job aids is return-on-expectations or ROE (Hodges, 2001). ROE is another means of determining the

Noted

Evaluating a job aid that has been bundled with other interventions (or even other job aids) is a little trickier but still very manageable. Under these circumstances, it's important to identify at the outset a specific task or skill that the job aid is specific to. You should also look for ways to isolate the impact of the job aid. Isolating the impact of the job aid is not too difficult if implementation of the job aid is staggered across the organization.

impact of a particular intervention or defining the ROI. To gauge the ROE, the designer asks the client to identify what improvement has occurred since the rollout of the job aid. The designer asks the client's opinion what percentage of that improvement is attributable to the job aid. That percentage of improvement can then be used to identify the organizational value or even ROI.

It is important that the designer doesn't ask leading questions. However, if this process is done in an evenhanded manner without leading questions, the results tend to be very credible within the organization because the source (the client) is usually regarded as credible about these numbers.

Noted

If you are going to use ROE, you must use a very open and unbiased approach to gathering your data from the client. If you are perceived as asking leading questions or trying to provoke positive responses, then your ROE data will lack credibility within the organization.

Getting It Done

Now that you've completed this chapter, it's time to do some thinking about how to apply what you've learned. Try your hand at exercise 7-1.

Exercise 7-1. Evaluating job aids.

1. Think of an instance where it would make sense to disseminate a job aid to only part of the work-force. For instance, different locations and limited resources make it unlikely you could give it to everyone with the required support simultaneously, thereby creating a natural control group. How might you use this control group to help in your evaluation of a job aid?

2. Review one of the job aids you've developed in an earlier exercise or use one of the job aid examples from this book. Identify which of the five evaluation levels would be appropriate to use in evaluating that job aid. How would you go about conducting the evaluation?

3. What do you see as the most challenging organizational barriers to evaluation within your organization for any job aids you develop? How could you overcome those obstacles?

4. What evaluation knowledge and skills do you need to improve so you can effectively evaluate the job aids you produce? How will you acquire those competencies?

In the concluding chapter, you'll examine the most common mistakes designers make with job aids and think about ways you can use job aids to not only close performance gaps in your organization, but also help with your own work, as well.

8

Avoiding Common Mistakes

What's Inside This Chapter

Here you'll learn about:

▶ The most common mistakes job aid designers make and how to avoid them
▶ Ways you can apply what you've learned in this book
▶ Ideas for job aids you could start working on right now.

At this point in the book, you should have a very good idea of areas that are easy to goof up or some skills you want to polish so you don't get it wrong. Certainly this book has highlighted some elements, such as how important a legitimate trigger is to the job aid development process, that are critical to achieve success with job aids. If these elements are ignored or done improperly, they can mean the difference between success and failure.

The Most Common Errors

What are the most common mistakes designers are likely to make in creating a job aid? A diverse group of instructional designers, performance consultants, and trainers were asked exactly this question. The group consisted mostly of internal practitioners, but also included external consultants. All were experienced in the field. They identified a range of common job aid design mistakes:

▶ *Failure to provide the context with the job aid:* Too many designers don't provide an explanation about the purpose of the job aid or who should use it. This becomes especially important because even if you provide an orientation or initial training, there will inevitably be employees who miss it or are hired afterward and encounter the job aid "cold" so it needs some explanation as to purpose.

▶ *Failure to actually observe the process or performer:* Relying solely on interviews or documentation results in a limited task analysis that is likely to be missing critical information. Trust what your SMEs tell you but verify through observation.

▶ *Failure to focus the job aid:* Instead, some designers create a job aid that combines several tasks or procedures, resulting in a job aid that is not specific and is sometimes too cumbersome to use for just one task. If you have a legitimate trigger or a good task analysis, you should have no trouble producing a specific job aid that is tightly focused.

▶ *Use of cumbersome, unnatural mnemonics on the job aid:* Acronyms or abbreviations that form the basis for a job aid should fit naturally rather than being forced. Many designers build acronyms into their job aids to aid with memory. To produce a cute word that is memorable, too many job aid acronyms end up requiring letters that are silly or not on point with the task. To get a good acronym, the designer sometimes resorts to words that weakly associate with the task, producing a job aid that emphasizes the wrong skills or lessons in the interest of producing a memorable acronym.

▶ *Failure to plan for evaluation during the initial client engagement meetings or the early stages of the process:* Too often designers jump into the task and consider evaluation only as an afterthought. This problem is exacerbated by clients who generally want to rush on to the next problem. If you've done your analysis work well, it behooves you to evaluate the impact of your work; job aids can produce some very high ROI numbers.

▶ *Failure to consider job aids often enough as a solution for soft skills issues:* Job aids as a solution for technical skills performance problems (such as product details or correct procedure) is almost a no-brainer. But, performance consultants often don't think of job aids to help with such soft skills issues as how managers can solicit feedback or ways to keep meetings focused. The tendency is to throw more expensive solutions, such as training or coaching, at the problem rather than use job aids.

▶ *Failure to integrate job aids closely enough to the necessary task:* This means that the performer must either stop work or move from the worksite to get to the job aid. Consequently, using the job aid becomes a hassle and it is usually easier to just try to muddle through without the job aid.

▶ *Failure to provide a simple, easily accessible repository for job aids:* The job aid by itself is fine but it ends up tucked away in a filing cabinet to be forgotten and never used because there is no intuitive storage for it that makes it easy to reach during the task. Job aids don't exist in isolation, but support just part of a performer's job. Therefore, you need to think about how the job aid is to be integrated into other job supports and how to make the job aid easily accessible.

▶ *Failure to provide supporting training:* Some job aids require training on how to use them. In other cases, the tasks they address are so complex that they must have instruction on using the job aid to get the task right. Such mistakes result in a job aid that collects dust or—even worse—causes confusion because performers can't figure out how to use it.

▶ *Failure to provide instruction on how to train to use the job aid:* In instances where the designer anticipates the need for training, too often there is no direction provided on how or what to train for the job aid. Given that the "trainer" in this case might be someone with technical knowledge but poor platform skills or little experience in training, this failure can be deadly.

▶ *Failure to simplify:* An ideal job aid includes plenty of different information (before-and-after information, purpose, warnings, and context). Ultimately, however, the purpose of a job aid is to make something difficult, easy. You must look for ways to be concise and precise.

Putting It All Together

Here is an opportunity to practice applying what you've learned in this book. This next section will provide a series of quick exercises and cases for you to build your skills and practice applying what you've learned.

The Scenario

You are an internal performance consultant for a firm that sells liability insurance for corporations and businesses. The majority of the employees in the firm operate from one central location, but there is frequent travel to client sites around North America. Most business is done by phone with employees (also referred to as agents) who contact organizations to discuss potential policies and take calls from clients to answer questions and troubleshoot problems with existing policies.

You have been contacted by one of the senior partners in the firm. She tells you, "We've noticed a trend: Over the past year, we've seen an increase in policy cancellations, which have cost the firm nearly $2.9 million in lost revenue not to mention the time the agents spent dealing with these problems. The firm has adopted new procedures for dealing with upset customers who call agents demanding refunds or requesting that their policy be canceled. The new approach is that when a customer contacts an agent demanding either a refund or a policy cancellation, instead of trying to solve it individually, the agent is to refer the client to a special customer care center we're setting up to deal with these problems. We think the new customer care center will be able to provide the expertise and attention to salvage these accounts because they will specialize in solving only these kinds of customer problems. We were going to call a meeting for everyone in the firm, but there are always too many people out traveling or on leave. So, one of the other partners said you could make a job aid to deal with this, and I wanted to see if that made sense to you."

Upon asking a couple of clarifying questions of the senior partner, she says, "Well, actually not all upset customers will be referred to the care center. Sometimes a customer may get upset in the midst of a conversation and make threats. The original agent should still deal with those situations, but we've found that when a caller initiates a call to us for the express purpose of demanding a refund or canceling, those calls are beyond the skills of most agents. Also, we've found that more than 90 percent of customers who call with the intent of canceling indicate this intention within the first 30 to 45 seconds of the call. Accordingly, if the request for a refund or cancellation comes in the first 45 seconds of the call, that qualifies as something that should go to the care center. The agents are too busy to deal with all of these cancellation calls; those situations require someone focused solely on dealing with complaints to have a good success rate at dealing with these kinds of upset callers. In any case, agents are going to have to exercise judgment on when to deal with the upset customer versus when to transfer the caller to the care center. Do you think we should use a job aid on the new policy?"

Your Challenge. Now, it is time for you to go to work. Is this a legitimate trigger for a job aid process or is this just a case of senior management deciding on a solution before anyone knows what the problem is? What's your decision? Should you agree with the senior partner or suggest that management consider other alternatives?

Expert Guidance. This is a legitimate trigger. The initial management plan was to hold a meeting to inform the staff of the new policy. A job aid can be a good substitute for a meeting because it also provides information.

Your Challenge. The first phase of the job aid development process is to collect task and performer data. Because the solution involves providing information to the agents about a new policy ("When someone calls in seeking a refund or to cancel, transfer the call to the care center"), do you think it's necessary to conduct a task analysis? You have several questions you need to resolve. Does this situation even call for any kind of a task analysis? If so, who would you want to interview or observe and what questions would you need to get answered?

Expert Guidance. Yes, a task analysis is necessary. You need to know more about the performers, their work situation, and how the task of answering calls is handled before you can design the job aid. Because this seems like a relatively simple set of instructions (agents will transfer anyone who wants to cancel a policy or demand a refund to the care center), as long as the agents know how to transfer the phonecall, what task analysis would be necessary? But, you've created a new task here because agents currently don't have to evaluate calls to determine if they should be transferred to the care center. There might be barriers to doing it as easily as management thinks, but you won't know this until you conduct a task analysis and get a better sense of the work setting. Therefore, a task analysis is necessary.

What information will you need to do your task analysis? You will want to observe and than interview an agent who is an accomplished performer, but you'll also want to read any policy manual or official process for handling customer calls. And you will need to talk to senior management to get confirmation about what specific calls are to be transferred to the call center and what the criteria is for such

Think About This

Sometimes a task analysis involves more than one employee, especially if there is a process that involves a handoff (one person passing work to another). Don't think that a task analysis is limited only to the steps provided by one performer. Typically, a task is owned by one particular performer, but you might find instances when two or more workers do different steps within the same task.

calls. Depending upon the technology and procedure involved for transferring calls to the care center, you might also need to talk to a telecommunications specialists to be sure you have the correct steps involved in switching callers to the center.

Your task analysis discovers the following details:

▶ The phone system used by the agents indicates if a call is internal (from another employee) or incoming (outside the firm and, therefore, almost always a customer). The phone system would indicate that a customer call is internal if it is being transferred by another agent.

▶ All agents are expected to answer incoming calls with a short greeting, the name of the firm, and his or her name, followed with "How may I help you?"

▶ After the initial welcome and greeting, the agent is supposed to ask if the caller is from a company that holds a policy with the firm.

Think About This

An accurate and complete task analysis might require talking to the workers "upstream" or "downstream" of the performer in question, that is, the people who receive work from or hand work off to the agent. Oftentimes, a task breaks down when work is handed off from one performer to another in the larger process. Additionally, you may discover that there are critical steps your performer must take in the task and that the person best able to identify how critical they are is the worker who receives the handoff from your performer.

▶ If the answer to the previous question is yes, then the agent is supposed to ask for the caller's name, company affiliation, zip code, and policy number. The policy number and company name are the critical information. The other data is only for customer record purposes and to confirm that the call is legitimate. If the caller is unsure if the company has a policy, the agent may search by company affiliation.

▶ Agents are permitted to answer internal calls with their own name only.

▶ Until this change in procedure, agents were authorized to deal with any caller (new and existing clients). Additionally, agents were expected to deal with any concerns, problems, upsets, or questions from any new or existing customers. Therefore, agents were expected to have a wide range of skills and a comprehensive knowledge of the various policies.

▶ When they call, clients at times are angry or demanding something from the initial interaction in the call. Sometimes clients are calm at the start of the call and become angry or frustrated later in the conversation.

▶ If clients have questions or problems with their existing policy, an agent can call up policy details on the screen from the customer database, but it takes time to access the database and then additional time for the agent to become familiar with the details of the individual policy.

▶ Senior management's explanation of the new policy is that any caller who initially indicates a desire to cancel or seek a refund is to be asked to hold and then be transferred to the care center. No other questions or data are to be collected from that customer. However, any caller who does not initially indicate the desire to cancel or seek a refund but does so later in the conversation is to be handled by the agent or the agent's manager. Senior management's rationale is that if the caller didn't initially indicate this desire (to cancel), then it may have been a result of the conversation with the agent—something that the care center would need to carry on the conversation. Therefore, the agent would be better informed in how to deal with the client and would already have the customer's policy called up on the screen.

▶ You are told by agents that "management is always changing the greeting and call processing policies around here. We all have a hard time keeping it straight. The running joke is 'If it's Monday, we must have a new script.'" And, you hear employees making cracks about the "greeting of the day."

▶ There is no formal documentation of this task either in policy manuals, orientation, or employee training. There appears to be wide variance in how agents actually handle incoming calls, how callers are greeted, and agent demeanor.

▶ The new customer care center has no expectations of calls transferred from agents other than the call should be transferred after the agent discovers the desire for a refund or cancellation. The care center staff does not want the agent trying to mollify the customer first and then transferring the call.

Your Challenge. The next stage of the process is to confirm that a job aid is an appropriate solution for this performance problem. You need to be sure that this is a problem due to information or memory issues. Given that senior management has concluded that agents don't have the skills to adequately deal with this type of caller (one demanding a refund or cancellation), is this the right intervention? Determine if this is a performance problem appropriate for a job aid or if it calls for another category of solution?

Expert Guidance. This problem is indeed appropriate for a job aid. Remember, the problem with the upset callers isn't going to be solved by the job aid (an information solution). It is going to be addressed by the newly created care center (a combination knowledge and process solution). The purpose of the job aid is to inform the agents of the shift in procedure and remind them of it as they perform their daily routine answering calls. Therefore, the job aid addresses an information and memory issue with performance.

 Noted

Clients don't usually do a root cause analysis on problems. They are likely to attribute a cause (or solution) to a problem without having really analyzed why the performance gap is occurring. So, it isn't enough to go on a client's hunch that the employees have poor memory or just need a reminder; the failure to perform could be due to a host of other problems that more information will not solve or overcome.

Your Challenge. The next phase involves determining what training support is necessary. Will the job aid require training support so performers can use it and, if so, what kind of training?

Noted

Perhaps it seems impossible to determine if the job aid requires training when you haven't even designed the job aid yet. Nevertheless, this determination is driven in large part by the task analysis insights. The information you've gained about the task, performer skills, and work environment will help you decide whether or not training support is necessary.

Expert Guidance. No training or orientation is necessary. If you use job aid 4-1 (in chapter 4), you can see that no training is indicated. The job aid, if designed well, is likely to be intuitive enough to stand alone. An email to all employees announcing the development of the care center and the existence of the new policy is required so that the presence of the job aid makes sense. However, this is an implementation feature of the care center initiative. The job aid itself calls for no new skills by the performers in question, nor is there any indication at this point that critical information necessary to use the job aid can't be contained on the job aid itself.

The next phase in the process involves picking the appropriate format for the job aid. Because it covers what agents are and aren't supposed to say to certain callers, should it be a Script job aid? If agents need to decide which calls to keep and which ones to transfer, isn't a Decision Table format most appropriate? If there is a mandatory sequence of actions required, perhaps that makes a Step job aid a better fit. Because the message is so simple ("Transfer all initial refund/cancellation requests to the care center"), then perhaps a Reminder format is best.

Your Challenge. Now it's time for you to decide which format would be the best for the new job aid. Use job aid 3-1 (in chapter 3) to help you choose the appropriate format.

Expert Guidance.
There are several job aid formats that might be appropriate in this situation. However, the best format is likely to be either a Step job aid or a combination

Step/Decision Table format. That's because the critical parts of this change to the task (answering a client call) involve two important elements: transferring initial problems to the care center (timing and sequence are important) and distinguishing between calls to keep and calls to transfer, requiring a decision by the performer as to which approach is appropriate.

The next phase in this process involves designing and developing a prototype of the job aid. Because the agents take most calls at their workstations and also need to call up customer data on their computer screens, might this be a job aid that is best integrated into the software as a pop-up screen or pull-down menu? Perhaps it would be more effective as a paper product that can be attached the side of the cubicle. If it's a simple piece of information, then it could be displayed as a screensaver that runs continuously on the computer monitors when they're not in use.

Your Challenge. Design and develop a job aid that addresses this performance issue.

Think About This

Designing the right job aid is more than just phrasing the information correctly on a particular media format. You need to keep in mind the work context. What else is going on around the performers that could influence their willingness to use the job aid or their ease at accessing it during the task? The context and environment are critical considerations as you choose what media to use, how much explanation to provide, and what the job aid itself will look like.

Expert Guidance. This problem probably calls for a job aid integrated into the client software or computer that the agents use. However, because this book is paper, you'll get an opportunity to review a paper copy of a job aid solution to this problem (job aid 8-1).

Notice several important elements on this job aid:

1. It has a date or version number on it. This matters because agents told you that the phone policy changes constantly. Agents are likely to have several copies of memos and scripts floating around and won't be sure which policy

---

JOB AID 8-1. Procedure for handling customer calls.

Procedure for All Incoming Calls
Ver. 1.0   12/12/05

This is the procedure that all agents are to use for all incoming calls from customers and all transferred customers.

Warning: If a customer asks for a refund or to cancel a policy in the first 45 seconds of the call, indicate that the customer care center will help him or her, then transfer the call to the CCC at extension 123.

Step 1. Answer with "This is (name) with Antioch. How may I help you?"

If the customer says...	...then...
"I want to cancel my policy"	Indicate that the customer care center will help him or her. Then, transfer to CCC at ext. 123.
"I want a refund"	Indicate that the customer care center will help him or her. Then, transfer to CCC at ext. 123.
Any other response	Process the call.

Step 2. Ask the customer if he or she currently holds a policy with Antioch.

Warning: It is critical to get a policy number and company affiliation from callers.

If the customer answers...	...then...
"Yes"	Get: • Caller's name • Company affiliation • Zip code • Policy number
"Unsure"	Search the database by company affiliation.
"No"	Ask the purpose of the call.

Step 3. Initiate the client-needs analysis process. Any requests for cancellation or refunds after the first 45 seconds are **not** transferred but dealt with by agent.

version is correct. You'll want to identify your job aid so users can tell it is still current (either with a date or version number).

2. The job aid includes more information than is necessary to decide whether to transfer a call to the care center. Why? Because if the job aid is going to be appropriate only after the task (answering the call) has started, the performer is likely to either have to interrupt the task or be extremely polished to be able to integrate it. By designing the job aid so that it starts at the beginning of the task (answering client calls), it becomes more likely the agent will rely on the job aid for the critical aspect of the task—transferring appropriately to the care center.

3. Notice the combination of both Step and Decision Table formats in this job aid. Also notice that the steps are numbered and each decision was enclosed so it was clear which conditions lead to which outcome.

4. There were also several warnings that performers needed to know either before proceeding or beginning the process. Those warnings were highlighted and put before the relevant step.

The next two phases in the job aid development process are to validate the draft job aid and then troubleshoot any problems. Because these two phases may be iterative (as you create a draft, seek feedback, make changes, seek feedback, make changes, seek feedback, and so on), they'll be treated together for this performance problem. You'll need to think through how you're going to get feedback on your prototype. This is more than just asking a few people, "So, what do you think?" Once you get the input that you need, you may need to adapt the job aid. In some cases, these changes will be minor. In other instances, it may mean junking the original design and going with a different approach. In some cases (such as with EPSS approaches or job aids embedded within a tool), it might not be possible to junk the design; you might have to seek ways to do the best job you can to adapt what you have so it's workable.

Your Challenge. What should your validation process look like, whom should you seek input from, and what potential troubleshooting issues should you anticipate?

Expert Guidance. You will want input from several different methods. Because this is a new policy from management, you should show the job aid to a senior manager authorized to interpret the new policy. You need that manager's approval to ensure

Think About This

Sometimes the validation process involves more than just potential users. For instance, you might want to run the prototype by management or legal affairs or HR to confirm that it is compliant with directives or company policy.

that the job aid does accurately reflect the policy. You'll also want to show it to some agents to get their reaction. Ideally you'll be able to observe several agents use the job aid. You might even consider using the equivalent of a mystery shopper, in this case, a staged caller who pretends to be a client seeking a refund. Also, it would be worth running it by someone from the customer care center to get feedback as well.

As for likely troubleshooting issues, your task analysis should have raised several red flags. Given that the job aid will be used in a cubicle, next to a computer and phone in an office that likely generates a lot of paper, there are probably going to be issues with the job aid "disappearing" under other memos. Even if the job aid isn't buried under paper, it could easily be separated from the phone area where it needs to be during calls. The frequent changes in phone policy encourage agents to ignore messages about new policies because they likely assume it will change again in another week. It also means it is difficult for agents to keep track of which policy is current.

Either in anticipation of these issues or in response to your validation efforts, you likely would have done some of the following:

▶ Provide some way to track version control of the job aid (such as an issuing date).

▶ Attach the job aid to the phone or the side of the monitor screen, or create a small stand or "message tent" so that the job aid is both visible and difficult to stack things on.

▶ Identify some way to check that the job aid is being used, perhaps by having managers walk around and observe or tracking incoming calls to the customer care center.

The last two phases of the job aid development process involve rolling out the job aid to the users, as well as maintaining and upgrading the job aid. Information gained from the task analysis as well as the validation phases is very informative at this point. Your knowledge of the performers and their work environment can give you valuable insights into how to implement the job aid and avoid potential booby-traps. Once the job aid has been put in the performers' hands, you'll also need to be sure that you have a plan to maintain access and quality (as job aids wear down, break, or need replacing) as well as upgrades (as there are changes to the task because of job redesigns or policy changes).

Your Challenge. How should you implement this job aid and what do you need to consider in terms of revisions and support?

Expert Guidance. You already know from the trigger that initiated this process that it isn't possible to bring all the performers together to announce the changes to the task, introduce the job aid, and answer questions. Therefore, information needs to come out through other means. Additionally, you know that this task has changed so frequently in the past that the agents have had trouble keeping track of what the correct policy is for answering calls and dealing with caller issues. This means that it is imperative that you build in communication strategies to get the word out and confirm that the agents are clear on the change as well as the job aid. As part of this, it is critical that the messages that go out are aligned and use the same reference; otherwise, they could be interpreted by users as even more changes (rather than confirmation of the earlier memo). Here is what a possible roll-out plan might look like:

- ▶ Meet with and inform all frontline supervisors of the change in policy. Answer any questions about the change and provide them copies of the job aid. Inform the supervisors that they will be expected to follow up after the job aid is provided to determine if it's been used and encourage agents to depend on it.

- ▶ Send out emails to all agents to inform them of the change and the implementation date, and let them know to expect the job aid.

- ▶ Meet with all agents who can attend a 30-minute orientation. Explain the changes, provide copies of the job aid, and answer any questions. Any who can't attend are mailed their job aid and a supervisor follows up with a phone call.

- ▶ Have several "mystery shoppers" call in to demand refunds to see if agents follow the new policy.

Think About This

If you discover that the task goes through frequent changes, you need to either make it easy to replace the job aid or create a design that allows for modifications.

▶ Encourage supervisors to walk around and observe agents.
▶ Follow up with an email and then some spot visits to individual agents to get their input on the job aid.

As for the maintenance and upgrade of the job aid, you have two good groups of candidates to handle storage of extra job aids: the supervisors and the customer care center staff. Both groups have an incentive to make sure the job aid is in the hands of the employees and is used appropriately. Because this is a white-collar workforce, the job aid will face different wear and degradation issues than it would if the work environment was blue collar or was taken on the road. You will also want to account for turnover rates as you figure out how many job aids to produce. That the company policy for this task keeps changing implies that you won't need to produce many surplus job aids.

Think About This

Although it isn't imperative to produce all the copies of the job aid in one run, you do want to try to estimate approximately how many job aids you'll likely need and then try to produce them in one or two batches. The reason for doing this is that any time there is a gap between production runs, small variations creep into the job aid. You may decide to move the logo just a little or change the font of the header. The graphics shop may use a slightly different color of paper. The programmers may use a different version of the program to write the code or produce graphics. In any case, the job aid will often appear different from one batch to another. Performers than tend to notice the difference in appearances, assume the first job aid is now obsolete and toss it, thereby depleting your job aid supply.

The upgrade of the job aid needs to be discussed with the client at the very beginning of the development process. In this instance, you will want to track at least two items: the change in behavior of the agents when dealing with a refund or cancellation demand and the overall impact on refunds/cancellation rates. The latter should be easy to measure. It is something the organization would likely track anyway and it should give you an indication of what business impact the job aid had. The first will likely require observation of a group of performers. This observation not only gives you the information you need to determine how much the job aid changed performance, it also gives you insight into how to upgrade the job aid. What you will likely discover is that the next version of the job aid will probably include some language prior to transferring the call to prepare the customer for the call center experience and what to expect.

Getting It Done

At this point, you need to look at how to apply your knowledge about job aids. There has never been a better time to be skilled in developing job aids than the present. Organizations need to do things faster. Job aids are a possible solution for that challenge as job aids can usually be developed quicker than many alternative interventions. As we see a more competitive world, performance and accountability are being emphasized. Job aids are a critical intervention in the battle to close performance gaps.

So, what steps can you take to improve your skills and confidence in designing job aids? The exercises and questions at the end of each chapter in this book are a good start. With any book it's too easy to skip the application and work, focusing just on the text. If you skipped any of the exercises, now is a good time to go back to them. Additionally, you can start with your own needs. Look at something in your personal life (such as the maintenance schedule for your car, a checklist for backing up files on your computer or checking for viruses and spyware, a data array of emergency addresses, or a job aid to help you pick investment opportunities). Build your confidence by starting with material that matters to you and that you will use.

You'll also want to identify the skills and knowledge you want to improve if you're to be strong at designing job aids (exercise 8-1). This book is not an introduction to performance analysis (and, therefore, front-end analysis or performance diagnostics), nor is it intended as a detailed look at evaluation. For these reasons, you might find it helpful to get more expertise in either of these areas, which will prove useful beyond job aid work. Gaining expertise in task analysis is invaluable. Try starting with a modest task analysis involving some chore or project at home to get a better feel for this iterative process while building your confidence and skills. Take a look at the references listed in the back of *Job Aid Basics,* and you'll discover a range of resources that were not only sources for this book, but also are great ways for you to build your expertise with job aids.

Now that you've had an opportunity to complete this book, the most valuable thing you can do is to practice applying this knowledge right now. Look for potential job aid projects at work. Don't wait for permission or a request to provide a job aid; identify ways for you to build your confidence and expertise on this subject. As you gain confidence and develop your own skills, you'll feel comfortable recommending a job aid as a possible intervention. What's more, others will notice what you've done.

Practice some of the parts of the job aid development process. *Use what you've learned. All of these are strategies that will lead you to improve your ability to produce effective job aids.*

Exercise 8-1. Putting job aids to work for you.

1. The list of common errors included in this chapter would make a good Reminder or Checklist you could use as you work on a job aid project. To improve your practical application of the material in this book and reduce the likelihood of you making any of these errors, think about converting the material from the list into a job aid of your own. It will give you practice developing a job aid and you'll have a resource to help you avoid these mistakes with your work.

2. Reviewing the work you've done on job aids in this book, what aspect of the job aid development process do you think you're weakest at? What can you do to improve your ability in that area?

3. Think of an upcoming project where a job aid might be a viable option. How can you sell the job aid option to the client?

(continued on page 144)

Exercise 8-1. Putting job aids to work for you (continued).

4. Besides SMEs, what resources could you access that could be helpful for future job aid development projects?

5. What job aids and tools can you create for yourself to help you the next time you have a job aid development project?

References

Gautier-Downes, J., and A. Rossett. (1991). *A Handbook of Job Aids.* San Francisco: Jossey-Bass/Pfeiffer.

Harless, J. (1986). "Guiding Performance With Job Aids." *Introduction to Performance Technology,* 106–124. Bethesda, MD: International Society for Performance Improvement.

Harless, J. (1996). "Great Ideas Revisited." *T+D, 50*(1): 52–53.

Hodges, T. (2001). *Linking Learning and Performance.* Boston: Butterworth-Heinemann.

Kirkpatrick, D.L. (1975). *Evaluating Training.* Alexandria, VA: ASTD Press.

Long, C. (2004). *Job Aids for Everyone.* Amherst, MA: Human Resource Development Press.

Lovell, J., and J. Kluger. (1994). *Lost Moon: The Perilous Voyage of Apollo 13.* New York: Houghton-Mifflin.

Phillips, J. (2003). *Return on Investment in Training and Performance Improvement Programs.* Burlington, MA: Butterworth-Heinemann.

Piskurich, G. (2000). *Rapid Instructional Design.* San Francisco: Jossey-Bass/Pfeiffer.

Sanders, E., and S. Thiagarajan, S. (2002). *Performance Intervention Maps.* Alexandria, VA: ASTD Press.

U.S. Coast Guard. (2003, November). "Job Aids." *Standard Operating Procedures for the Coast Guard's Training System, 4.* Washington, DC: U.S. Coast Guard Headquarters.

Additional Resources

■■

Campbell, C. (1996). "Job Performance Aids." *Journal of European Industrial Training, 20*(6): 3–22.

Chase, N. (1997, December). "Job Aids When Memory Fails." *Quality, 36*(12): 96.

Colvin-Clark, R., and C. Lyons. (2004). *Graphics for Learning: Proven Guidelines for Planning, Designing and Evaluating Visuals in Training Materials.* San Francisco: Jossey-Bass/Pfeiffer.

Elsenheimer, J. (1998, October). "Job Aids in the Technology Age." *Performance Improvement, 37*(8): 32–35.

Elswick, J. (2001, May). "Performance Support Shapes Training Programs." *Employee Benefit News, 15*(6): 39–42.

Franklin, M., and J. Rossi. (2001, August). "On-the-Job Aid for Caregivers." *Kiplinger's Personal Finance, 55*(8): 82–83.

Hale, J. (1998). *The Performance Consultant's Fieldbook: Tools and Techniques for Improving Organizations and People.* San Francisco: Jossey-Bass/Pfeiffer.

Hubbard, A. (2004, July). "Determining the Scope of Training." *Mortgage Banking, 64*(10): 110.

Lohr, L. (2002). *Creating Graphics for Learning and Performance: Lessons in Visual Literacy.* Upper Saddle River, NJ: Prentice-Hall.

Mager, R.F. (1984). *Preparing Instructional Objectives.* Belmont, CA: Lake Publishing.

Reynolds, A. (1998, January/February). "Job Aids: Still a Performance Support Essential." *Technical Training, 9*(1): 6–7.

Rossett, A. (1998). *First Things Fast.* San Francisco: Jossey-Bass/Pfeiffer.

Russell, S. (1997, November). "Create Effective Job Aids." *Infoline* no. 759711. Alexandria, VA: ASTD Press. http://store.astd.org/product.asp?prodid=1360&deptid=.

Salopek, J.J. (2004, July). "Balancing Work and Learning." *T+D, 58*(7): 16–19.

Spaulding, K., and F. Dwyer. (2001). "The Effect of Time on Task When Using Job Aids as an Instructional Strategy." *International Journal of Instructional Media, 28*(4): 437–448.

Tufte, E. (1990). *Envisioning Information.* Cheshire, CT: Graphics Press.

Tufte, E. (2001). *The Visual Display of Quantitative Information.* Cheshire, CT: Graphics Press.

Zielinski, D. (2000, January). "The Shape of Things to Come." *Training, 37*(1): 26–36.

About the Author

■ ■

Joe Willmore is president of the Willmore Consulting Group, a performance consulting firm located near Washington, D.C. He has more than 25 years of consulting experience with a wide range of organizations including the World Bank, Intelsat, Lockheed Martin, the U.S. Navy, Booz Allen Hamilton, the National Geographic Society, and the Smithsonian Institution. He has served on ASTD's board of directors and held other leadership positions within ASTD and other professional societies. His work has taken him to Russia, Turkey, Greece, the Caribbean, and Central Asia. He currently serves as one of ASTD's facilitators for the HPI certificate series.

Joe Willmore is the author of *Performance Basics* (ASTD Press, 2004) as well as *Managing Virtual Teams* (Chandos Press, 2003). He was also a contributor to *What Smart Trainers Know* (edited by Lorraine Ukens, Jossey-Bass/Pfeiffer, 2001) and *HPI Essentials* (edited by George Piskurich, ASTD Press, 2002). In addition, he has written numerous articles for ASTD's *T+D* magazine and other publications, as well.

Joe Willmore lives with his wife and son in Northern Virginia. When he isn't working, he's usually kayaking, playing soccer, or breeding amphibians. He may be contacted at Willmore@juno.com.

About the Author

Joe Willmore is president of the Willmore Consulting Group, a performance consulting firm located near Washington, D.C. He has more than 25 years of consulting experience with a wide range of organizations including the World Bank, Intelsat, Lockheed Martin, the U.S. Navy, Booz Allen Hamilton, National Geographic Society, and the Smithsonian Institution. He is the author of *Performance Basics* (ASTD Press, 2004) as well as *Managing Virtual Teams* (Chandos Press, 2003). He was also a contributor to *What Smart Trainers Know* (edited by Lorraine Ukens, Jossey-Bass/Pfeiffer, 2001) and *HPI Essentials* (edited by George Piskurich, ASTD Press, 2002). In addition, he has written numerous articles for ASTD's *T+D* magazine and other professional publications.

"There is no better way to reduce training costs and increase training effectiveness than a well constructed job aid, and no one better to explain how to do it right than Joe Willmore. This book is a must for every trainer's bookshelf."

GEORGE PISKURICH
Consultant
Author, Training Basics (ASTD Press) and Classroom Facilitation: The Art and the Science

"An essential resource for anyone who needs to design and develop effective job aids from start to finish. *Job Aids Basics* has hit the mark as a comprehensive guide packed with a wealth of practical tips and examples. This book is a 'must-have' for anyone working in a performance consulting, instructional design, or training role."

LAUREL ROSINGER
Instructional Designer
Booz Allen Hamilton

"Whether you are a performance professional or someone just starting to develop job aids, this book is the complete resource for you. It will help you think through all the critical issues, concepts, and steps that you need to develop job aids that really work. The job aid examples, expert guidance, gems of wisdom, practice activities, and exercises will provide the job aid developer with the tools they need to be successful."

CYNTHIA DENTON-ADE
President
CDA Performance Systems

ASTD Press

1640 King Street   Box 1443
Alexandria, VA 22313-2043 USA

Tel *800.628.2783*   *703.683.8100*
Fax *703.683.8103*

www.astd.org

ISBN-13: 978-1-56286-415-6
ISBN-10: 1-56286-415-7

52995

9 781562 864156

110604 $29.95 (U.S.A.)